The Sociology of Children's Rights

The Sociology of Children's Rights

Brian Gran

polity

First published in 2021 by Polity Press

Polity Press
65 Bridge Street
Cambridge CB2 1UR, UK

Polity Press
101 Station Landing
Suite 300
Medford, MA 02155, USA

ISBN-13: 978-1-5095-2784-7
ISBN-13: 978-1-5095-2785-4 (pb)

A catalogue record for this book is available from the British Library.

Library of Congress Cataloging-in-Publication Data
Names: Gran, Brian, 1963- author.
Title: The sociology of children's rights / Brian Gran.
Description: Cambridge; Medford, MA : Polity Press, 2021. | Includes
    bibliographical references and index. | Summary: "Does the idea of human
    rights fail to protect the most vulnerable among humans: children?"--
    Provided by publisher.
Identifiers: LCCN 2020025659 (print) | LCCN 2020025660 (ebook) | ISBN
    9781509527847 (hardback) | ISBN 9781509527854 (paperback) | ISBN
    9781509527885 (epub)
Subjects: LCSH: Children's rights. | Sociology. | Human rights.
Classification: LCC HQ789 .G686 2021 (print) | LCC HQ789 (ebook) | DDC
    323.3/52--dc23
LC record available at https://lccn.loc.gov/2020025659
LC ebook record available at https://lccn.loc.gov/2020025660

Typeset in 11 on 14 pt Sabon
by Fakenham Prepress Solutions, Fakenham, Norfolk NR21 8NL
Printed and bound in Great Britain by CPI Group (UK) Ltd, Croydon

For further information on Polity, visit our website:
politybooks.com

Contents

Acknowledgments

The Sociology of Children's Rights arises from seemingly non-linear experiences. In many ways, my journey to crafting this text began in my youth. In primary school, a young man was "bused" from a school across the city to the suburban school I attended, but I was not bused to his school. In secondary school, although my friends and I were "up to no good," as my mother would say, the police officers who monitored our high school harassed my friends but left me alone. These experiences caused me to wonder whether government authorities were treating young people differently due to their skin color, gender, and family income. Weren't we entitled to the same experiences?

I want to acknowledge people who have deeply influenced this book. Nancy Davis challenged me to think sociologically about how and why rules serve some individuals and simultaneously present obstacles to others. Frances Hill taught me how a young person's right to due process works. Under Mary Ann Henderson's tutelage, I learned children's rights can be swept under the rug because young people are easy to overlook, especially in the family home. Ted Marmor, Mark Schlesinger, and Martha Minow encouraged my fascination with understanding why rights seem less useful when it comes to private domains, which Charles Ragin and Art Stinchcombe empowered me to study with methodological and theoretical rigor. The influence and teaching of these teachers are foundations to the questions I ask in this book.

During my first academic job, I observed a lawsuit a therapist filed against a religiously conservative "home" for firing her because she is a lesbian. The boys living in this home had been removed from their families; the therapist counseled the boys about these changes and the traumas they had experienced. The home's directors told the boys that the therapist's counsel and advice were the words of the Devil. During the publicity and politics around the lawsuit, the boys' interests were forgotten. I wondered if this scenario could happen in other countries; I checked and discovered it could and did. Two graduate students, Lynn Falletta and Robin Shura, and I gained access to a meeting of the European Network of Ombudspersons for Children (ENOC). ENOC members would only allow us access to their meeting if we promised to work hard to ensure the United States ratify the UN Convention on the Rights of the Child (UNCRC). They were not joking, and I took their charge seriously. Our interviews became conversations, which I am fortunately able to continue with Margrét María Sigurðardóttir, former Ombudsman for Children of Iceland, and Reidar Hjermann, former Ombudsman for Children of Norway. These experiences and exchanges prompt formulation of the question at the heart of this book: Why are children's rights needed if young people possess human rights?

I am grateful to Polity and their experts, including Jonathan Skerrett, Karina Jákupsdóttir, Leigh Mueller, and others, who have shaped and clarified the ideas presented in *The Sociology of Children's Rights*. I am grateful to Sarah Forner, whose input made a world of difference. I have learned a great deal from students at both Case Western Reserve University and Reykjavik University, who have never refrained from asking hard questions. I thank colleagues associated with the Reykjavik University Law School and Case Western Reserve's Sociology Department, Law School, and Schubert Center.

Further, I am grateful to Agnes Lux, Karl Hanson, and Patrick Thomas for stimulating this work. In many ways, I benefited from time spent with members of Iceland's Office of the Ombudsman for Children, especially Margrét María, Auður Kristín Árnadóttir, Eðvald Einar Stefánsson, and Elísabet Gísladóttir.

Countless friends have helped shape this book; I especially thank Bandana, Bjørn, Bryan, Cary, Chris, David, Joachim, John, Keri, Liz, Mark, Mary, Paul, Sandy, and Sue. My research has received support from the US and Iceland Fulbright Commissions, the British Academy, the Swiss National Science Foundation, and the US National Science Foundation.

Most of all, I thank my family – friendly critics who have influenced my thinking in countless ways. I thank Mary Beth who has patiently supported this book and other endeavors. I thank Søren and Elsa who were willing to code the UNCRC and otherwise put up with their father, including helping with this book. Thank you. SDG

Introduction

Through this book, *The Sociology of Children's Rights*, we will employ sociology to study children's rights. A sociological perspective enables us to go beyond rights on paper to think about how rights matter to young people. We will consider international treaties that state children's rights, the institutions societies have established to implement children's rights, and whether and how children's rights matter to young people. As we approach children's rights as part of an international framework, we will try to answer the question of whether we truly take children's rights seriously? First, however, a short story.

A story

It's the first day of school. You are the new student; your parents and you fled to this country before the fighting started. Your parents said that when the electricity and water stopped, it was time to go. Here you are, nearly 5,000 km away, and life is dramatically different. Not only are you "the new kid," you are learning a new language. Your parents are taking you to a building where you practice your religious faith with others from your country, although it is a warehouse from Monday through Friday. Your parents are having trouble finding the food you can eat. Some of the kids tease you because of how you dress. You are discovering that your new country looks, works, and smells very different from home. You miss your sister.

Your 14-year-old sister insisted on staying behind. She said she wants to mind the family business. You think she stayed behind to be with her boyfriend, who is 15 and whom your sister wants to marry. Back home, she can marry him next year. You worry that your sister will be forced into the military, or worse. You miss her and wish she was with you. You worry that you may never see her again.

Today, though, is the first day of school. Your school day started with a talk given by an ombudsperson. This ombudsperson explained to the students that they possess rights. He organized games for students to play to learn about rights. The ombudsperson talked about a children's rights convention and praised the United Nations. In your home country, the UN is ridiculed and people think it is weak, albeit dangerous. At home, teachers never taught about children's rights; you had never heard of an ombudsperson. The ombudsperson said that every child has the right to be safe, to grow up with food and an education, and to live with their families. Before he left, he handed out pencils to every student. On the pencil is a telephone number any child can telephone if they think their rights, or another child's rights, are being violated. Could this ombudsperson help your sister?

Young people arriving to new countries is common. For 2019, the UN estimates over 272 million people migrated, which is 3.5% of the world's population. Of these international migrants, 1 in 6 were people aged 20 and younger (United Nations 2020: www.un.org/en/sections/issues-depth/migration/index.html). According to UNICEF and the International Organization for Migration (IOM), of the 870,000 refugees who arrived in Europe in the year 2015,

20% were children (IOM and UNICEF 2015). For the year 2014, 23,000 asylum applicants to the European Union were unaccompanied young people (IOM and UNICEF 2015). These young people traveled without parents or caretakers. Reasons why young people travel without adults are time-sensitive. More than 23,000 asylum applications were made for young people just to Sweden for 2015, more than the 2014 total to the European Union (IOM and UNICEF 2015). For the month of October 2015, this number for Sweden was 9,300. Given recent events, these numbers may be higher and – depending on your perspective – worse.

Many young people grow up in dire circumstances. Harsh situations are compounded when young people do not have access to social services that are crucial to their futures, such as health care and education. Many young people experience malnutrition. UNICEF (2015) indicates that half of the deaths of children aged 5 and younger are attributable to under-nutrition. Many do not have access to drinkable water and sanitation. Almost 10% of the deaths of children aged 5 and younger are due to unsafe water and lack of sanitation. Even in societies where young people possess rights to shelter, food, health care, and education, many young people do not have those rights enforced. Young people who do not live with and grow up with their parents are not uncommon, too. UNICEF estimates approximately 15.1 million children are "double orphans," both parents having passed away (UNICEF 2017: www.unicef.org/media/media_45279.html).

Many young people will probably grow up in a family that is broken. In our story, parents and the son live in one society while the daughter lives in another. Most national governments agree that young people should grow up with their families; most societies have established norms addressing at what age a young person can live on her own (Feldman and

Quatman 1988). According to the UN Convention on the Rights of the Child (UNCRC) – the text of which can be found in Appendix 1 – governments are not to interfere with a young person's family (Article 16). If the young person is separated from her family, the child has a right to family reunification (Article 22). As a young person's right, this Article has received great attention, given historical precedent of military conflicts and wars that foment separation of children from their parents. This Article has generally not received the same attention when parents do not share households, such as circumstances where parents split up. Do young people possess a right to grow up in a household with all parents present? In the situation of break-up between parents, such as marital dissolution, does a young person possess a right to grow up with both parents if it is in their best interest? If so, how is a right to grow up with a family implemented? These questions, which may at first seem outlandish, are real. They challenge children's rights. On paper, even if young people are entitled to rights, do those rights matter to their daily lives?

Why sociology?

Why are we studying a sociology of children's rights? What is sociology of children's rights? Before I try to answer this question, let's spend a moment talking about what sociology is. Simply put, sociology is the study of society (Romero 2020). As a social science, sociology's cousins include anthropology, economics, geography, political science, and psychology. How is sociology distinct from these disciplines? One difference is that sociology typically focuses on people doing things together (Becker 1986). While many sociologists are interested in what people do alone, their primary interest is in what people do together, whether as a pair (a 'dyad'), a bigger group (a 'triad' is three or more people), a community, people who live within a country's borders, or people who cross national borders. From your friend and you to all people of the world, sociologists want to understand what we do together, how we do things together, where we do things together, and why we do things together (or not).

What is interesting about what people do together? Think of how different you are from your best friend or a family member. No matter who you are or where you live, life is different. Every day, life is different across the world. No person has the same "day" as anyone else. Even people who go to the same school, who attend the same physical education class, and eat lunch during the same period – their experiences are not the same. Even when two people are in the same room listening to the same lecture, what they hear and experience can be drastically different (Darling-Hammond, Flook, Cook-Harvey, Barron, and Osher 2020). How can all of us have different experiences when we share time and space?

Even when we share time and space, our experiences can be vastly different. Our backgrounds shape our beliefs and values. The socio-economic situation of our family affects where we live and whether we have enough food to focus on schoolwork. The societies in which we live can strongly communicate that our skin color and gender open and close doors to opportunities (Collins 1990). Backgrounds, situations, experiences, and understandings not only can vary across students within a single classroom, these social factors can and will change over the course of our lives.

Yet, in many ways, societies do their best to ensure our days *are* the same. Across the world, we organize days according to expectations and schedules. Whether sunrise is the start of the day or we are on our way to work and school by 8:00 a.m., we have set up rules that shape how we live together. Our institutions teach us right from wrong, including what it means to be "late." These structures, institutions, and rules help us develop social groups (Stinchcombe 1965). We often see the same people on campus. We make friends in the classes we attend and get to know people who study the same subjects. We notice when a student is "new." We come to recognize people who ride the same bus each day, and notice when a rider is new to our bus. How and where we spend our time in society often identifies who is and who is not a member of our society.

Societies have set up, as well as inherited, obstacles that stop people from doing things together. Take citizenship. Citizenship is often thought of as the status of holding a national passport. Some sociologists, on the other hand, approach citizenship as the status of being a member of a society (Janoski 2012). A person can hold a national passport, but experience isolation and exclusion from institutions and experiences essential to societal membership. In our story, the boy and his parents have migrated to the host country. They probably do not possess a passport of that host country. Given that they are getting to know, and learn how to navigate, new cultural practices, they may feel they are not members of their new society. In fact, people who already live in the host society may not want them to feel they are members.

As well as needing to learn a new language and standing out as "different" by the way he dresses, the boy in our story is also different in a way that we might not immediately be conscious of. The boy is a member of a social group that many societies have designated as different: he is a young person. Many societies have developed norms of what childhood is supposed to be (Thorne 1993). By establishing norms of childhood, societies are distinguishing young people from other societal members. Societies make childhood a part of what our lives are supposed to be. By doing so, childhood becomes a period of a person's life that is distinct from the rest of the person's life. Sociologists want to understand how childhood is constructed similarly and differently across societies (Qvortrup 2014). What is supposed to be part of childhood? What is a "bad" childhood? How do societies foster "good" childhoods? Do societies place high priority on ensuring that a family stays together? How does a society define a family?

Even though she is age 14, the sister of the boy in our story lives in the sending country. She tells her family that she wants to maintain the family business. Her brother fears that she will be conscripted into the military. In many societies, a good childhood does not include military conscription. Indeed, human rights treaties forbid military service until age 18. Staying in the home country may make the boy's sister vulnerable to long working hours, inability to obtain formal education, and military conscription. The boy anticipates that he will grow up without his sister. Situations in which families are split up due to violence concern sociologists (Wakefield and Wildeman 2013).

Sociologists want to understand how and why societies are organized in ways that leave some groups vulnerable to crises (Wilson 1987). As human beings, everyone is vulnerable to bodily harm (Turner 2006). Members of some social groups, however, are more vulnerable to disease, disaster, and other dangers (Link and Phelan 1995). For these social groups, their vulnerability may arise from disadvantages they face. A social group may be vulnerable to disease because available housing is near environmental hazards. Some groups are vulnerable to disaster because their neighborhoods are built on weak infrastructures. Other groups may be vulnerable to economic distress. Some groups of workers are more likely to face long-term unemployment when economies undergo recessions, causing families to lose their homes. These losses may lead to decisions to move from neighborhoods and school districts. In these and other societies, outcomes parents experience are rarely viewed from the perspective of young people. Should society intervene so that young people do not experience dislocation and disruption in their families' lives? Young people's interests and rights are often ignored.

Members of some social groups are excluded from social locations and processes used to change society. Young people, as a group, are excluded from political arenas (Sloam and Henn 2019). They are not permitted to vote and run for office. Instead, the thinking is that the adult takes into account the child's best interests when casting her vote (Grover 2010). This supposition ignores conflicts of interests between adults and young people. An adult may prefer to pay fewer taxes, but those taxes may be needed to bolster the young person's educational opportunities.

Sociology offers crucial insights into how and why people experience children's rights. Sociology can offer evidence of why some young people possess and exercise rights. And why some young people do not.

Why children's rights?

Key objectives of human rights are to promote equality, eliminate discrimination, help people living on society's margins, and remove vulnerabilities (UN Population Fund 2005). Not one human rights treaty only applies to adults. Instead, the documents that together are often called the International Bill of Human Rights – which are the UN Declaration of Human Rights, the International Covenant on

Economic, Social, and Cultural Rights, and the International Covenant on Civil and Political Rights – apply to all people. Their terms are universal.

Why do we need children's rights? Why are human rights inadequate? That's a great question, and we will tackle it in the pages of this book. But let's start here. First, why not just focus in this book on human rights? One answer is that children's rights are the perfect means to determine whether human rights truly are meaningful. Human rights are universal: they are supposed to be available to everyone. Human rights reduce marginality: they are supposed to help people who live in the margins move into mainstream society. Human rights prevent vulnerability: they are supposed to ensure social, economic, and political security. These three aspects of human rights – non-discrimination, inclusion, and security – are goals we have for all young people. Why do we think human rights are not up to the job of ensuring the well-being and interests of young people?

As a group, young people should benefit from each of these components of human rights. Because they are universal, human rights should benefit young people. In fact, by insisting that human rights are "good enough" for young people, we are merely insisting that human rights apply to young people. Young people are the same as anyone. Insisting on children's rights implies young people face inequality and discrimination that adults do not.

If human rights reduce marginality, why do we need children's rights? Because they reduce marginality, human rights should ensure young people are members of mainstream society. Children's rights, ironically, mean that young people need more than human rights. Possessing children's rights does not mean young people are precluded from human rights. Young people, the logic goes, need human rights *and* children's rights. We will examine whether children's rights promote societal inclusion of young people.

If human rights mitigate vulnerability, why do we need children's rights? Because they reduce vulnerability, human rights should ensure that young people enjoy protections against crises. Thinking through how children exercise their rights, we recognize that young people must typically rely on adults. Ironically, this reliance may lead to vulnerability. To exercise their rights, children must rely on adults.

If we think for a moment whether young people are endowed with human rights, we may conclude that young people *do* need children's rights. Young people are kept at the margins of society. They are legally prohibited from politics, able neither to vote nor to run for office. Societies are organized in ways that force young people to depend on adults. Adults have set up institutions and rules that keep young people on the margins in other ways. In many societies, young people are legally precluded from gaining full-time, paid work because they are required to stay in school. Decisions about what school to attend are typically made by adults, not the young person receiving the education.

We organize societies so that young people are placed in vulnerable positions. Young people cannot exercise many – perhaps any – of their rights without others' support, a fact with which most adults do not have to deal. Young people are dependent on adults to implement their rights. The UNCRC states that young people have rights to health care (Article 24), food (Article 24), and education (Article 28), among other rights. To use these rights, an adult must assist – sometimes enable – a young person to exercise the right. An adult must register a young person before the medical provider can see the child as a patient. In many societies, young people are legally incapable of signing contracts, including leases, which are needed to obtain shelter. If a child requires legal protection, in many societies she is legally incapable of hiring a lawyer or seeking a court's protection without an adult's assistance. To implement the right to an education, a young person must enroll in school. Enrolling in school is typically undertaken by an adult. This arrangement of rights for young people can exacerbate a child's marginality and vulnerability when the young person is legally attached to an adult who does not have access or ability to purchase health care, food, and shelter. This predicament is made worse in societies that do not consider young people's welfare to be a societal responsibility.

Sociology of children's rights

Sociology of children's rights can reveal patterns and complexities in how societies "do" young people's rights and how young people experience those rights. On paper, children's rights are universal, inalienable, indivisible, interdependent, interrelated, and non-discriminatory. Children's rights are tools to be used to advance young people's interests, especially their well-being. Yet evidence suggests the failure of children's rights.

Children's rights are often overlooked and ignored. Why? The experiences of the boy in our story are telling. He learns about his rights and the UNCRC from a children's ombudsperson. The office of this children's ombudsperson was probably established by the national government, which provides the office's budget and regulates the office's work. In contrast, many people living in his home country where his sister remains have not heard of children's rights or an independent children's rights institution. They think poorly of the United Nations and its treaties. Having learned that children's rights are universal, and that the children's ombudsperson has the job of ensuring that young people enjoy their rights, the boy wonders whether the ombuds-person can help his sister. The answer is "no"; from his investigations, the boy will learn that the children's ombudsperson's jurisdiction is limited to his host country. No independent children's rights institution can transcend national boundaries.

The UN Committee on the Rights of the Child is responsible for monitoring national governments' efforts to implement the UN Convention and was established in 1991. Committee members are from States parties. Their terms run for four years. Members' backgrounds vary, from law to psychology to social work to medicine to government and non-government organizational work. While the Committee possesses the power to insist that member states work to ensure that, as a group, young people possess and can use their rights, until 2014 the Committee could not work with individual young people. The Committee was legally incapable of hearing petitions of individual young people. This restriction meant that the Committee was powerless to intervene in a violation of a child's rights.

The UN Committee can now hear individual cases. In April 2014, the Optional Protocol to the UNCRC on a Communications Procedure entered into force. A key feature of this optional protocol is that it permits the UN Committee to receive and consider individual complaints. This approach to receiving and hearing individual complaints, however, has weak impacts, at best. First, the UN Committee can consider complaints from an individual only if that young person's national government has ratified the Optional Protocol to the Convention on the Rights of the Child on a Communications Procedure. As of November 2019, 46 national governments had ratified this optional protocol. From a young person's perspective, only if this young person lives in one of those 46 countries, not in one of the other 147 member states, can she file her complaint with the UN Committee.

What power does the UN Committee have to respond to the young person's complaint? After hearing the complaint, the UN Committee can recommend to the child's national government that it take action to remedy the complaint. The UN Committee's power is limited to making a recommendation.

While this change to being able to hear individual complaints should not be downplayed, in effect the UN Committee is returning a young person and her complaint to the society from which the complaint likely emanated. The UN Committee is counting on a child's national government to enforce that young person's rights. This process of a complaint traveling from the child's society to the UN Committee and back to the child's society seems empty. It highlights the ineffectiveness of a young person's rights.

Where we are headed

The next chapter will introduce approaches to the sociology of children's rights, then discuss what children's rights are from a sociological perspective. The profession of law and the social science disciplines of anthropology (Reynolds, Nieuwenhuys, and Hanson 2006), geography (Aitken 2015), political science (Therborn 1996), and psychology (Melton 1980), among others, and the humanities, including history (Sealander 2003), philosophy (Matthews 1996), and religious studies (Hashemi 2012), have made valuable contributions to studies of children's rights. What can sociology contribute to our understanding of children's rights?

Starting with its unit of analysis, sociology concentrates on young people as a social group (Hernandez 1993). With a focus on young people's rights, sociologists strive to examine all aspects of young people's lives. Sociologists have studied education and play of young people (Thorne 1993). Sociologists examine impacts of social structures on inequities and inequalities shaping young people's lives. Sociologists study exclusion of young people, including prohibitions on working in formal economies (Balagopalan 2014), limitations on voting and forming parties in political systems (Gran 2011), and restrictions in influencing institutions that shape their lives. Sociologists have studied how educational institutions shape young people's welfare and fail to meet young people's present and future needs (Raudenbush 2012). This research is particularly important given emphases in some countries on formal education as a means of reducing inequalities and promoting opportunities. Sociologists have studied young people's lives in the family home and in other institutions (Lareau 2011), including schools and religious institutions (Ammerman 2006). Sociologists have studied young people's labor, paid and unpaid, as well as their military conscription (Close 2014). Sociologists pay attention to the weak trust young people hold in "mainstream" institutions, including governments (Marsh, O'Toole, and Jones 2007). Sociologists have studied violence against, and committed by, young people, and its impacts (Sharkey, Tirado-Strayer, Papachristos, and Raver 2012). Sociologists have taken perspectives of parents, caretakers, teachers, and others who shape young people's lives. Most importantly, sociologists have taken perspectives of young people in making decisions about managing their lives and planning their futures (Edin and Kefalas 2005).

When studying young people's rights, an important approach sociologists and others have taken is a child-centered perspective, of which different types exist, which takes the child's perspective on interests, needs, and rights when studying young people's circumstances, and institutions in which they live (Ridgely 2011).

Why children? Why their rights? As a group, children are understood in various ways: as deserving protection, as innocents, as worthwhile investments of human capital, and in other ways (Aizer and Cunha 2012). One key attribute of young people as a group is that they are not adults. When studying children's rights, by implication we are distinguishing young people from adults. As a consequence, children's rights denote rights that are distinct from others' rights. Are those rights adults' rights? We rarely discuss rights as belonging to adults, not to young people. Does the notion of human rights implicitly mean adults' rights? Otherwise, why create a new category of rights belonging to children?

Chapter 1 will then consider sociological underpinnings to rights. In particular, are rights socially constructed, or do they exist outside social relationships (Gregg 2011)? This question especially is important to children's rights. Do children's rights exist on their own, or because governments endow children with rights (Freeman 1998)? Why does this question's answer matter? This question is one that continues to rise to the top of battles over young people's rights, including in conflict with parents' rights, or when government leaders make choices to reduce commitments to social programs that appear to weaken implementation of children's rights (Dwyer 1994; Hertel and Libal 2011).

Through chapter 1, we will undertake an analysis of international agreements on children's rights, from formation of the 1924 Geneva Declaration of the Rights of the Child to ratification of the UN Convention on the Rights of the Child and regional children's rights treaties, such as the African Charter on the Rights and Welfare of the Child. A touchstone of children's rights is the United Nations Convention.

Adopted in 1989, this UN treaty is often considered to be the most widely supported human rights treaty, with only the United States not having ratified this convention (UN 2015). This chapter will compare the UN Convention with regional treaties, including the African Charter and the European Convention on the Exercise of Children's Rights.

Chapter 1 will focus on what rights are labeled as children's rights. It will contrast what rights are considered specific to young people, compared to adults – for instance, the right to an education. A key conception of rights is a bundle of rights. When rights are interrelated and interdependent, experts believe rights are more effective and foster societal membership. This chapter will then turn to predominant typologies of rights, such as Wesley Hohfeld's (1917), to identify which types of rights are more widely available to young people, and which types are not (Fortin 2009; Mortorano 2014).

For over a century, institutions have been built to develop, implement, and enforce contemporary notions of children's rights (Alston and Tobin 2005). Chapter 2 examines these institutions, the barriers they have encountered, and the work they have achieved (Shier 2001). This chapter will examine institutions that have been established to monitor and advance young people's rights (Gran and Aliberti 2003; Thomas, Gran, and Hanson 2011). Chief among these institutions are committees set up in regard to a specific treaty. A paramount example is the UN Committee on the Rights of the Child. Tasked with monitoring implementation of the UNCRC and its optional protocols, the UN Committee consists of 18 independent experts from across States parties (Woll 2000). This chapter will examine the work of these experts, especially their General Comments, and evaluate their impacts on young people's rights and interests. One General Comment that will receive particular attention is General Comment no. 2, which deals with roles of national independent human rights institutions in advancing young people's rights.

Another type of organization this chapter will examine is these national independent human rights institutions. More particularly, this chapter will examine the goals and work of independent children's rights institutions (ICRIs), sometimes called children's commissioners and children's ombudspersons (Linnarsson and Sedletzki 2014). Understood as independent of governments, ICRIs play key roles in advancing young people's rights, yet are neglected in academic studies of children's rights and interests. Many national governments have established ICRIs (UNICEF 2013). These ICRIs typically have the objective of monitoring national governments' efforts to implement the UNCRC, and national legislation to advance young people's rights. This chapter will examine where these ICRIs are established and prominent roles they have played in children's rights advancement.

A third type of institutions will be examined: powerful nonprofit organizations that advocate for and against young people's rights (Cohen 1990). This discussion will consider these organizations' histories, their current membership and funding structures, and how they work to reach their objectives (Seneviratne and Mariam 2011).

It is difficult to separate institutions from politics of children's rights. Chapter 3 examines three sites of political conflict: international–national, national, and individual children's cases. At the international–national level, this book examines interactions between the UN Committee and representatives of national governments, as well as other actors, such as child advocacy groups. At the international–national level, what prompts struggles to advance young people's rights? Or to define rights? How are these struggles resolved? The UN Committee and representatives of national governments and other actors negotiate over not only fulfillment of rights, but which rights are deemed essential and to what degree they must be enforced. For instance, why is the right to health care considered essential? What aspects of health care must a national government secure to young people (Chinkin 2006)?

At the national level, this book examines national politics of children's rights. It will examine instances of conflict between groups advocating for children's rights and groups advocating against children's rights. For instance, in some countries, parents' rights groups have formed in response to UNCRC ratification steps, as well as in response to enforcement of particular rights of young people, such as young people's freedom of conscience. Some opponents point to weakening of parent–child relationships. Over what rights of young people do conflicts arise? What are their arguments?

This book will examine politics of children's rights at a local level through examination of specific rights, including the right to education. This discussion will consider methodological and data challenges to studying young people's rights at the local level. In addition, it will synthesize findings of studies at local levels to identify recurrent weaknesses in young people's rights, and reasons for those weaknesses.

While international treaties and national laws declare young people's rights, unclear is how those rights matter to young people (Waibel 2014). Chapter 4 examines how young people understand and use rights. It will examine whether rights can undermine interests of young people. A right can have multiple meanings to a young person. A right may enable a young person to overcome exclusion to become a full member of a community (McCluskey, Riddell, and Weedon 2015). A right may enable a young person to pull an institution's levers that open doors to resources and opportunities (Osler and Osler 2002). A "bundle of rights" (Marshall 1949) may empower a young person to change relationships and circumstances. A right to freedom of conscience may enable a young person to think differently about life, relationships, and community (Langlaude 2007).

Yet a right may have little meaning to a young person. Young people may be unaware of rights that, on paper, they possess. In our story, an ICRI informs the students about their rights. Our hero's sister, who stayed behind, may be unaware of the rights the UNCRC affords her. Even as our hero becomes aware of his rights, he may conclude that rights are not relevant to the life he lives. Resources needed to exercise rights may not be part of young people's lives (Archard 2014a).

A young person may view rights as belonging to *other* young people (Balagopalan 2014). Our hero may come to think that rights belonging to citizen students are taken more seriously than his rights as a refugee. Even among citizen students, some young people may conclude that their rights are worth less because of skin color, sexuality, disability, or other factors. Institutions through which young people can exert their rights may be beyond reach, not exist, or be set up to fail young people (Chunli 2006). A right may be ineffective to a young person whose crucial needs are not met. Our hero does not know that, although his country of residence has ratified the Optional Protocol on a Communications Procedure, his home country has not, meaning that neither he nor his sister can bring an individual complaint to the UN Committee on the Rights of the Child.

Rights may not be appealing. A young person's beliefs and practices may be in opposition to rights (Boyle and Preves

2000). Rights may remove a young person's authority and autonomy. A young person's right to education has been inter-preted to mean not only a right to a free, public education, but that this education is compulsory. A long-term concern is that a young person is required to use this right, which can limit choices (Abbott and Breckinridge 1917). Being compelled to attend school means that the young person cannot perform work during school hours. Young people may view rights as containing contradictions. They may understand these rights as imposed by institutions and actors who are unfamiliar with – or, worse, opposed to – the young person's opinions and values (Pupavac 2011).

Young people may interpret rights as ironic. Young people may recognize that public debates and conflicts over children's rights indicate that young people's rights threaten some actors. Young people may recognize a mismatch between public dialogues and their personal experiences. They may conclude that failures to advance their rights indicate they are not full members of society (Fieldhouse, Tranmer, and Russell 2007). In some societies, rights of young people may be criticized as being more generous than rights of adult citizens.

Efforts to implement children's rights often proceed without considering what children's rights are able to accomplish (Reynaert, Bouverne-De Bie, and Vandevelde 2012). Chapter 5 examines evidence of impacts of children's rights on children's interests and well-being. Beyond important unto themselves, do children's rights matter to young people (Guggenheim 2005)? Which rights matter?

Further, chapter 5 investigates whether advances in children's rights have positive repercussions for adults (Alderson and John 2008). A set of opposite questions has been asked. For example, do strong women's rights advance young people's rights? Chapter 5 will turn around this question to ask whether widely available and strong young people's rights benefit others. If so, how?

Given that children's rights typically are believed to matter within nation states, does evidence indicate that young people's rights have cross-national consequences? Previous scholarship, such as the World Society approach, has examined factors responsible for diffusion of young people's rights. This chapter will investigate whether young people living in one nation state benefit from living next-door to young people who enjoy extensive rights (Bentley 2005). How can rights practices in the country where our hero has taken refuge influence practices in his home country, where his sister continues to live?

This chapter will conclude with an examination of children's rights that are "missing." Major treaties on children's rights, such as the UNCRC, seem to constrain debates of futures of children's rights. Rights not included in these major treaties appear to be beyond debates over children's rights. As a result, scholars, researchers, and activists, as well as government and UN officials, have implicitly narrowed our perspectives of what rights belong to young people.

This constraint not only is a mistake – it undermines young people's interests. Just as our notions of young people change over time and vary across societies, new rights and overlooked rights must enter into global perspectives of young people's well-being. An important example is the right to enjoy benefits of scientific progress and its application. This right is featured in the International Covenant on Economic, Social, and Cultural Rights. Until the last ten years, however, the UN and States parties to the Covenant largely overlooked this right. Young people stand to benefit a great deal if their human right to science is enforced, yet the UN Committee on the Rights of the Child has not approached this right in its work with States parties.

Chapter 6 considers why some governments, institutions, and actors contend that children's rights are wrong (Guggenheim 2005). What contentions are made about failures and dangers of children's rights? Are these arguments specific to groups of young people – for instance, infants who rely on adults (Freeman 2000)? Or do these arguments pertain to young people of specific regions or nations (Salazar-Volkmann 2005)? As an example, some government officials suggest that rights have western qualities, making their application to non-western children inappropriate, at a minimum. Some scholars and researchers object to expending resources on children's rights when funds are tight and, they say, other needs are more important. Another argument may be that children's rights will cause more harm than good when exercised in some types of legal systems, such as systems employing adversarial approaches (Guggenheim 2005).

This chapter will deliberate on impacts of these arguments regarding qualities of children's rights. After all, if any of these arguments take hold, are children's rights truly universal, inalienable, indivisible, interdependent, interrelated, and non-discriminatory? Do we truly take children's rights seriously?

CHAPTER I

What Are Children's Rights?

Introduction

Yesterday you learned that you possess rights. In fact, the ombudsperson explained that a UN convention declares all young people possess rights, no matter where they live. The ombudsperson said that every child has the right to be safe, to grow up with food and an education, and to live with their families. You had never heard about these rights at your previous school, let alone your previous country. You wonder what other rights the convention says belong to you and your sister. How do you find rights that belong to you?

Where do we find children's rights? Are children's rights socially constructed, or are they separate from social interaction (Gregg 2011), part of the natural order? Do children's rights exist on their own or because governments endow children with rights (Freeman 1998)? The lattermost question continues to rise to the top of battles over young people's rights. It is raised when children's rights seem to conflict with the rights of their parents. Can a young person choose her religious beliefs or must she attend church because her parents insist? What recourse do young people have when government leaders reduce commitments to social programs that appear to weaken children's rights (Dwyer 1994; Hertel and Libal 2011), such as cutbacks to public education (but not to public pensions)?

A touchstone of children's rights is the United Nations Convention on the Rights of the Child (UNCRC). Adopted in 1989, this UN treaty is often considered the most widely supported human rights treaty, with only the United States not having ratified this convention (United Nations 2020). Through UNCRC ratification, national governments not only indicate their support of children's rights, they state their intention to ensure that children's rights matter. This chapter examines major international treaties that have shaped children's rights. What do these treaties say about their rights?

Children's rights are sometimes characterized as forming a *bundle* of rights (Barnes 2012). A bundle of rights means that the rights are interrelated and interdependent. Rights work together – a collection of rights that together support and reinforce each other. Do young people possess a bundle of rights? Experts of human rights, including scholars and policy makers, say that possession of a bundle of rights is necessary to an individual's membership in society (Isin and Wood 1999). Is this conception applicable to young people: must young people possess a bundle of rights to be members of their society? If so, in practice, do young people possess a bundle of rights they can exercise (Fortin 2009; Mortorano 2014)?

Foundations of children's rights

From where do children's rights come? Foundations of children's rights are centuries – even millennia – old. These foundations shape contemporary notions of children's rights and how children's rights work. Young people's rights are articulated in religious texts. The Torah's Book of Deuteronomy, chapter 24, verse 17, provides protection and safeguards to young people, placing responsibility not only on parents, but on strangers. The Bible's New Testament attributes statements to Jesus that support children's rights to pursue their beliefs and live according to what their conscience directs. The Gospel of Mark, 10:14, states, "But when Jesus saw it, he was indignant and said to them, 'Let the children come to me; do not hinder them, for to such belongs the kingdom of God.'" Other New Testament Gospels, Matthew 19:13–14 and Luke 18:15–17 ascribe this statement to Jesus. Experts interpret the Koran as saying that parents are obligated to provide spiritual and material well-being to their children, as well as that children possess the right to receive fair shares of property from their parents. Children's rights and who owes duties to young people are identified in these religious texts. Parents are obligated to fulfill their children's rights, including spiritual education, as well as providing food and resources necessary to their child's education. Parents are not the only people who are obligated to ensure children's rights are implemented. Strangers, according to the Book of Deuteronomy and the New Testament, hold duties to young people, such as their protection. Responsibilities of ensuring young people's rights are implemented extend beyond the child's family. These ancient propositions are found in today's societies.

We can turn to philosophical traditions to find insights into children's rights. The philosopher, teacher, and politician Confucius concentrated on young people's well-being when it came to their rights. According to Confucius, if a father did not support his children's welfare, his children were entitled to disobey him (Huang 2013: 132). Aristotle's notion of the state continues to influence contemporary forms of and approaches to governance. At the heart of Aristotle's state is the male citizen (*Politics*, book I, part XII). The male citizen is central to how a state works with the community and with the family, including relationships within the household. According to

Aristotle, household relationships are organized distinctly around husband–wife and father–children. The husband is expected to rule constitutionally over his wife such that he treats his wife appropriately, so that she does not choose to vote him out of office. On the other hand, the father is to rule over his children as a king rules over his subjects. In Aristotle's conception, the state, consisting of male citizens, will intervene into the family home if the father does not govern his children correctly.

While Aristotle's conception of the state and politics shapes current approaches to governance, his ideas are not without criticism. A key objection is Aristotle's idea that male citizens, acting as the state, will intervene into the family home to challenge another male citizen's actions as husband/father (Benhabib 1999; Gobetti 1997; Minow 2003; Romany 1993). Given that the state consists of male citizens, these experts challenge the possibility that the state will intervene into the family home. More precisely, they contend that male citizens will not challenge another male citizen's governance, even when male citizens fail to govern properly. Critics (Gobetti 1997: 31) challenge structures of Aristotle's state, accusing this state as based on and promoting misleading assumptions on utilities of rights in private domains for groups whose members do not consist of male citizens, such as children. Today, governments of many societies fail to intervene into family homes to enforce young people's rights, even in cases of domestic violence (Minow 2003). Given the common application of Aristotle's state, we may question whether contemporary governance structures are set up in ways that permit violations of children's rights in private domains (Gran 2009).

Despite influences of religious beliefs and philosophical traditions, not until the late 1800s did children's rights receive significant attention. Widespread industrialization brought migration from rural to urban communities, and shifts from agricultural to industrial employment (Tilly 1983). While young people may have previously worked on farms, increasingly they were employed in factories. Attention was drawn to conditions in which young people were growing up (Tuttle 2018). Associations of people who shared interests in common causes were founded. While the American Humane Society – currently the American Humane – had concentrated its efforts on protecting animals, it began to advocate for the welfare of young people. The American Society for the Prevention of Cruelty to Animals took on a case of child abuse in 1873 (Pearson 2011). Pearson (2011), in her terrific book, *The Rights of the Defenseless*, describes the organization's efforts to establish legal protections for children's welfare. Pearson (2011: 4) demonstrates how the American Humane Society worked to establish "cruelty" to children as a problem that required changes in how societies function.

New kinds of evidence influenced perceptions of humanity and children's lives. Around the time the American Society for the Prevention of Cruelty to Animals was advocating for protections for children, photographers documented harsh realities in which young people were living and working in the United States. You may have come across the work of two notable photographers whose work changed our notions of childhood: Jacob Riis and Lewis Hine. Born in Denmark, Jacob Riis, who lived from 1849 to 1914, was a journalist who used his work to bring about social reform (Library of Congress n.d.). He drew attention to social crises of poverty, housing, and exploitation in New York City. His photographs both alarmed and led to reforms of these problems, particularly ones facing young people. Lewis Hine, an American who lived from 1874 to 1940, was a sociologist hired by the

National Child Labor Committee to document conditions in which young people worked. The photographs Riis and Hine took caught the attention not only of reformers, but of many people living in the United States. Riis promoted his findings through lecturing across the United States and other countries. Hine's work was primarily disseminated through a magazine called *The Survey*, which the National Child Labor Committee published. The social activism of the American Humane Society, and the reporting and photographs of Riis (see figure 1.1), Hine (see figure 1.2), and others, called attention to the destitution and dangers many young people experienced in the United States. The photograph Riis took probably is from 1888 and the one Hine took probably is from 1908.

Figure 1.1   Jacob Riis, *How the Other Half Lives* (1890)

Figure 1.2   Lewis Hine, *Exposing Child Labor in North Carolina, 1908* (1910)

The photographs not only challenged common perceptions of childhood, but understandings of responsibility toward young people. The photographs raised questions of whether and how individuals were responsible to strangers' children. Did everyone owe duties to protect young people and promote their welfare? In some countries, such as France, education and protection from hazardous work were understood as children's rights (Fass 2011). In most societies, however, a framework of children's rights did not come into existence until after World War I.

Bundles of rights

A right can be understood as a protected exercise of choice or entitlement (*Stanford Encyclopedia of Philosophy*, 2017).

A right can protect an important interest belonging to one person, but fulfilling that right requires another person to act or not act (Moyn 2016). Another person may have to provide resources through paying taxes or volunteering their time, such as serving on a jury. We usually expect state officials to ensure rights are enforced, as well as to decide between competing rights (Dworkin 1977). However, as we will see while examining children's rights, others are often considered responsible for protecting young people's rights. Parents and other non-governmental actors also are responsible for protecting and policing the rights of young people.

A classic conception of rights is T. H. Marshall's *bundle* of citizenship rights. In *Citizenship and Social Class* (1950), Marshall describes citizenship rights as a bundle of three types of rights: civil, political, and social (see table 1.1).

If an individual does not possess this bundle of rights, she will not enjoy her status as a citizen, a member of her society. For Marshall, citizenship is about membership. Marshall states, "Citizenship is a status bestowed on full members of the community" (1950: 28). He elaborates, "All who possess the status are equal with respect to the rights and duties with which the status is endowed" (1950: 28–9). These statements point to potential problems in Marshall's notion of citizenship.

Let's take a close look at two parts of Marshall's ideas. First, note that Marshall contends that citizenship is bestowed. He is unclear as to what or who bestows this status. Given that rights

Table 1.1 Types of citizenship rights

Marshall's three types of rights	Additional citizenship rights
Civil	Economic
Political	Participation
Social	Cultural

are exercised to make claims against government, citizenship is probably bestowed by government in Marshall's conception. Second, observe that citizenship is bestowed on full members. What constitutes a full member? According to Marshall, full members are individuals who possess citizenship rights. This point raises a concern about whether Marshall is employing circular reasoning. To become a full member of a society, one must possess citizenship rights. To possess citizenship rights, one must enjoy the status of full membership. Although these questions are incidental to what Marshall is trying to achieve, which is to argue that citizenship – full membership, in other words – is based on an individual possessing a bundle of three types of rights, they do point to conundrums for Marshall's ideas surrounding citizenship rights.

Nevertheless, Marshall's notion of a bundle of rights may offer insights useful to studying young people's rights. What Marshall had in mind for the bundle is that citizenship requires all three rights (Allars 2001: 80; Van Deth, Montero, and Westholm 2007: 1–3). Why would Marshall conceive of citizenship rights as a bundle? One reason may be that he conceived of citizenship rights as interrelated, interdependent, and mutually supportive. If a person has not enjoyed enforcement of her social right to education, she may not be able to read. A person who is not able to read may experience difficulties in completing an electoral ballot, as well as in distinguishing between misleading and accurate campaign promises. Likewise, a person who does not possess rights to job protection may encounter pressures from an employer on how to vote. These problems are not hypothetical. Mares (2015) documents employer intimidation of employees' voting in Romania and Bulgaria. Similarly, in the 2016 US presidential elections, US newspapers such as the *Washington Post* and the *New York Times* documented employer coercion of US employees' votes. This coercion effectively violates an individual's right to vote. If a person's social rights are strong, her civil and political rights will be based on a stronger foundation. If a person has a right to health care, a social right, she may be able to exercise her right to free speech or to vote. These rights must be instituted into law to have meaning and consequence.

Since Marshall introduced his famous ideas of citizenship, others have revised those ideas to incorporate additional types of citizenship rights. For example, a prominent sociologist of citizenship, Thomas Janoski, argues for the incorporation of participation rights (Janoski 1998; Janoski and Gran 2002). Janoski's conception of participation rights focuses on participation at the workplace. When it comes to participation rights, Janoski asks whether workers have the right to influence various aspects of work, ranging from the rate at which work is undertaken to working conditions. Others have extended Janoski's conception to further domains, such as schools. Participation rights in a school empower a young person to have a say in how her school functions. One way the right to participation in schools is implemented is through student government. Student government is a means by which, experts assert, students can shape the school's curriculum and administration (Lansdown, Jimerson, and Shahroozi 2014).

Other citizenship experts have incorporated economic and cultural rights into Marshall's conception of citizenship. Economic rights enable an individual to exert claims and interests in the marketplace (Kessler-Harris 2003). Economic rights include freedom from economic exploitation. This freedom entitles a person not to be taken advantage of in the marketplace. This includes during the performance of work, regardless of whether or not the individual was paid. Cultural rights are defined as rights to participate in and benefit from the cultural life of a community (Wang 2013). Cultural rights include the rights to learn a language and to preserve cultural traditions.

An important criticism of citizenship rights is that they are located in a vast system of inequality that, at the end of the day, does not empower individuals to change their socio-economic systems (Mann 1987). Citizenship rights enable an individual to try to make change within such a system. An individual's social right is exercised through what the welfare state offers. A civil right is tied to – indeed, is part of – an extant legal system. Critics question whether citizenship rights are useful tools for producing change in the circumstances of individuals who are not full members of their society (Spring 2018). All of these questions matter to children. Given that young people live in the societies their parents and other adults do, we should be able to assume that children enjoy citizenship rights. If they do, then why do we need children's rights?

Do citizenship rights matter to young people?

In his essay, Marshall does not distinguish between adults and young citizens. It is unclear whether Marshall would extend his concept of citizenship to young people. At the time in which Marshall wrote his essay, a person in the United Kingdom could not vote until age 21. On the other hand, public education was compulsory to age 15 (interest-ingly, military conscription started at age 18). Health care was provided by the National Health Service and available at birth onward. Given that Marshall conceived of citizenship as a bundle of interdependent, interrelated rights, it is likely that Marshall did not think of young people as citizens.

What are the ramifications of Marshall's excluding young people from his conception of citizenship? Marshall did not discuss the potential consequences of not holding citizenship – that was not the focus of his 1950 essay. What we can say with certainty is that Marshall considered citizenship to be key to societal membership. When it comes to young people, what does it mean to be excluded from societal membership? What is at stake in this exclusion?

Some experts contend that Marshall thought of young people as citizens in development (Cockburn 1998: 102; see Marshall 1950: 25). In this vein, as young people developed into citizens, they would begin exercising more rights over time as a means to prepare to fully exercise all rights. For instance, Marshall clearly conceptualized some social rights as crucial to a person becoming a citizen. As mentioned above, the social right to education is essential to a person's ability to exercise her civil and political rights effectively. Being healthy and accessing health care in situations of wanting to improve health is important in relation to a person's ability to exercise civil and political rights.

Some people and groups try to downplay the absence of the bundle of citizenship rights for young people by contending that an adult may represent a young person's political rights (Skelton 2010). Their perspective is that, although a young person's right to vote does not exist, an adult implements a young person's political interests through voting. The thinking goes that, while a child is "not old enough" to vote, a parent represents the child's interests when she votes. Because a parent loves and cares about and for her daughter, her vote will represent the interests of her child.

But what happens when a parent has two children, and those children's interests conflict? Or when a parent's interests, in the first place, conflict with those of the child? Can we count on an adult to act thoughtfully and deliberately on behalf of a child's interests and rights? Suppose the government of the jurisdiction where the child lives makes decisions about its budget, and this budget is limited, as they often are. Of course, a parent's interests may not align with her daughter's interests. A parent may oppose tax increases of any kind because of a tight family budget, or due to resistance toward government, or for a variety of other reasons. In analyzing this theory, even at the surface level, it becomes clear that a parent may not share the same values as her child.

This potential conflict in interest extends to all adults, including older adults. Across the OECD (Organisation for Economic Co-operation and Development) countries, the typical country spent 3.4% of its gross domestic product (GDP) on primary-to-non-tertiary (i.e., up to university) education in 2016 (OECD 2020). In the same year, the typical OECD country spent 8.2% of GDP on pensions: over 240% more. The typical defense for not contributing taxes to education – "I do not have children receiving an education" – can be applied to pensions: "I do not have parents to support." We can and should support older adults as they retire, but should we not extend similar support to young people as they pursue education and embark on careers?

The right to education is a key children's right, one reason being that Marshall is correct – a good education helps an individual effectively use other rights. Exercising the right to an education, however, depends on adults. In an analysis of 80 countries, UNESCO (2016) finds significant differences in educational experiences in terms of primary education. Completion rates for primary education range from 7% (Guinea-Bissau) to 14% (Chad) to 33% (Yemen) to 47% (Cambodia) to 61% (Bangladesh) to 82% (Colombia) to 100% (Kazakhstan and Montenegro). Although it is now dated, through its World Health Survey, the WHO finds for the period of 2002 to 2004 that 61.3% of males without a disability completed primary education, while only 50.6% of males with disability completed their primary educations. For women, the picture is worse. Only 52.9% of women without disability completed primary education. The report is much worse for women with disabilities. Only 41.7% completed primary education.

What stops young people from exercising their rights to education? Many factors might produce a satisfying answer to this question, but children's failures are rarely cited. Human Rights Watch (2019) concentrates on governments: "Behind this failure stands governments, which bear responsibility for ensuring that no child or young person is without education, and lack of focus – both in implementation and in content – in development agendas on governments' human rights obligations." The 2016 Human Rights Report on Nigeria published by the US State Department reports that many families favor boys over girls in deciding which children to enroll in school. This decision is made despite a Nigerian law that "requires provision of tuition free, compulsory, and universal basic education for every child of primary and junior secondary school age" (US State Department Human Rights Report 2016).

Marshall's conception of citizenship rights informs how many governments formulate rights belonging to their citizens. Marshall's citizenship rights have influenced notions of human rights that the UN has incorporated into human rights treaties, including the UN Convention on the Rights of the Child. Citizenship rights may theoretically fit young people, but, in practice, some citizenship rights may be beyond the reach of children. For some kinds of rights, young people must rely on parents, caretakers, and other adults to exercise their rights. This begs the following question: must children rely on adults to exercise all of their rights?

Hohfeld's typology of rights and children's rights

This analysis suggests young people's rights are often conditional on adults' decisions and abilities. This analysis raises questions for young people's rights. Are some rights dependent on another person taking a proactive step? Or refraining from taking a step? Are some rights belonging to young people designed to be contingent on another person's step or omission? A young person cannot usually enroll in school without support of adults, including parents and school administrators. An adult typically must help a young person escape exploitation. To assess these questions, we turn to a conception of rights developed by Hohfeld (1917).

Wesley Hohfeld was an American Law professor who lived from 1879 to 1918. In his lifetime, Hohfeld taught for various law schools before taking the position of Southmayd Professor of Law at Yale Law School (Oxford Index: *Routledge Encyclopedia of Philosophy*). Among his contributions, Hohfeld's conception is widely considered to be a crucial advance in analyses of rights.

Hohfeld organized his concept of rights into four components: claim, privilege, power, and immunity. According to Hohfeld, a claim is a right a person has to an item or service that a second person has a duty to provide. For a person to exert a claim successfully, resources are usually needed. Another person or entity has a duty to satisfy the claim. A child has a claim to an education, which teachers provide and taxpayers support. Yet some claims exist independently of another person's or entity's actions. As an example, a person can make a claim not to be subject to abuse. No one person must act, but this claim exacts a duty on other people not to abuse the other person. In this way, a claim corresponds to duties in more than one person. An important aspect of a claim is its focus on the duty holder. That person's duty is owed to the holder of the right. The aforementioned example of abuse demonstrates that a claim can require a duty holder to refrain from performing an action and that multiple people have this duty.

The next type of right in Hohfeld's concept is a privilege. According to Hohfeld, a privilege is a right to do something, if that is what you want, or not do something, if that is what you want. Another way to look at privilege is to conceive of it as an act that you do not have the duty to carry out. For example, in many societies, a person may possess the privilege of voting, but she is not obligated to exercise this right. In other societies, a person who maintains a license, whether to drive a vehicle or practice medicine, possesses a privilege. Yet this person is not required to drive or practice medicine.

The third right in Hohfeld's concept is a power. This Hohfeldian right enables the individual who possesses this right to change another's claim or privilege. In some societies, a parent may possess the power to direct her child to attend a religious service. In some societies, a government possesses the power to impose a curfew for the purpose of altering a person's privilege to move as she pleases.

The fourth type of right in Hohfeld's concept is an immunity. According to Hohfeld, an immunity is tied to a power. If a person possesses the right to change another person's circumstance, then the first person possesses a power, as we just discussed. If the first person does not have the ability to change the second person's circumstance, the second person possesses an immunity. If the second person possesses a right to prevent the first person from changing her circumstances, that right is called an immunity. A parent lacks the ability to force her child not to attend public school.

In many societies, the child possesses an immunity because public education is compulsory. This right to an education, which also is a claim, can serve as an immunity when a second person, such as a parent or employer, seeks to deprive the young person of her right to an education. Hohfeld's typology of rights may be useful to our study of children's rights. His typology may reveal that the four types of rights he identified are not necessarily part of rights available to young people.

Hohfeld and international children's rights treaties

Declaration of the Rights of the Child (1924)
Social reforms of the late 1800s and early 1900s seemed to point to the state's willingness to intervene into the family home and other private domains to secure children's well-being. These efforts tended to take place at the community and national levels. World War I was a watershed for children's rights. Consequences of the war were motivations to establish a new international agreement on children's rights. Eglantyne Jebb and her sister Dorothy Buxton established the Save the Children Fund, which eventually became the International Save the Children Union. Jebb and Buxton sought to protect and help young people who were caught in difficult circumstances of war, such as famine and disease. The Union prepared, then adopted, its own Declaration of the Rights of the Child. In 1924, the Union submitted this Declaration to the League of Nations. The League's membership was over 60 nation states from all over the world.

The 1924 Declaration was a monumental achievement: the first international agreement on children's rights. As a statement, a nation state's signature to the document merely indicates support of and agreement with the Declaration

(Cole 2009). As we will discuss, a convention or covenant obligates a national government to fulfill the treaty's provisions. Still, some governments did take steps to act according to the Declaration. French government officials posted the Declaration in schools, for instance.

Ironically, the 1924 Declaration does not use the term "rights." The Declaration identifies "states" children should experience. According to the Declaration, a child "must be" educated, fed, nursed to health, helped, sheltered, and cared for. The Declaration does not assert that a child possesses a right to an education. The Declaration declares that a young person should not be economically exploited, but it does not indicate that a child possesses a freedom from economic exploitation. The Declaration provides that a "backward child must be helped"; presumably, supporters of the Declaration would have wanted all children to participate in society and its cultural life. Further, the Declaration employs the language of responsibilities owed to children by their adult counterparts, noting that young people should not experience deprivation. Yet the Declaration does not indicate children are endowed with rights.

Despite the Declaration's name, failing to use the language of rights is problematic. The absence of this language suggests the Declaration does not define or position young people as full members of their societies. As we know, possessing rights is an indicator of societal membership (Marshall 1950; Williams 1992). The Declaration does not identify a bundle Marshall envisioned as citizenship rights. The Declaration fails to establish societal membership for young people.

Further, while some of Hohfeld's concepts can be detected, the 1924 Declaration does not use the terms associated with

Hohfeld's typology. Perhaps the most salient is Hohfeld's notion of a claim. Each component of the Declaration is stated in terms of a child receiving a good, service, or treatment. For example, a child who "is hungry must be fed," or a child must be the first to receive relief in a period of distress. The Declaration articulates expectations about social states, including health, shelter, and education, and economic rights, such as freedom from economic exploitation. While it may seem reasonable to hold that young people should experience states of health, shelter, and education, the Declaration does not clearly articulate these as *claims*. No one person is identified as bearing a responsibility to ensure that children experience these states, except that backward children should be helped. Instead, young people seem to possess immunities through the Declaration. Government actors and individuals, such as parents, should not deprive young people of being fed, nursed to health, or educated. Another person does not possess a power to deny a child of these states.

This implicit fuzziness between claim and immunity is exacerbated by the 1924 Declaration failing to use the language of rights. A right indicates "a clear legal obligation" a state owes to the young person. The 1924 Declaration fails to articulate a young person's right that would empower her to turn to government to ensure she is healthy, sheltered, and fed, gains an education, or is free from exploitation.

Unfortunately, the 1924 Declaration failed to protect young people. As people, including children, endured a second World War, it became clear that the 1924 Declaration did not have meaningful impacts. Battles, genocide and other atrocities, conscription of children into military and factory labor – all should have been prevented, but were not. The 1924 Declaration failed to prevent these harms to young people.

Rights	1924 Declaration of the Rights of the Child	Universal Declaration of Human Rights	1959 Declaration of the Rights of the Child	International Covenant on Civil and Political Rights	International Covenant on Economic, Social and Cultural Rights	UN Convention on the Rights of the Child
Binding?	No	No	No	Yes	Yes	Yes
Child	Not defined	Not defined	< 18	Not defined	Not defined	< 18
Nationality	No	Immunity	Immunity	Immunity	No	Immunity
Vote	No	Privilege	No	Privilege	No	No
Education	Immunity	Claim	Claim	No	Claim	Claim
Health care	Immunity	Claim	Claim	No	Claim	Claim
Economic exploitation	Immunity	Not clear	Immunity	No	Unclear	Immunity
Participation	No	Privilege	No	No	No	Claim
Culture	No	Privilege	No	Immunity	Privilege	Claim

Table 1.2 International rights treaties

The Universal Declaration of Human Rights

Shortly after its establishment, the United Nations adopted the Universal Declaration of Human Rights (UDHR; 1948). The UDHR, like the 1924 Declaration, is a declaration of principles. National governments that signed indicated their agreement with the Declaration's principles. The UDHR indicates human rights are universal, inalienable, indivisible, interdependent, and interrelated. Human rights are universal because they are for everyone. They are inalienable in that a person cannot relinquish them. They are interdependent and interrelated because one right is dependent on other rights (United Nations Population Fund 2005). These qualities mean that human rights are available to everyone, including children, and do not permit discrimination.

The UDHR states that everyone has a right to nationality (Articles 15 and 18). Everyone has a right to participate in their government and in elections (Article 21). The UDHR provides that everyone possesses a right to participate in cultural life (Article 27). All of these rights are expressed as immunities with which no other entity is supposed to interfere.

Aside from Articles 25 and 26, the UDHR does not discriminate between adults and children (see table 1.2). Article 25 states that all children shall enjoy equal social assistance. Article 26 articulates a right to free and compulsory education, a claim, but adds that parents have the right to choose their child's education, a power that has the potential to limit this claim. While the UDHR is a declaration of human rights that apply to everyone, including children, its terms indicate that the UDHR does limit young people's rights.

The 1959 Declaration of the Rights of the Child

Despite the UDHR's expression of universalism, including applications to young people, in 1959 the UN General Assembly adopted the Declaration of the Rights of the Child (see table 1.2). Given the existence of the UDHR, why did the UN adopt the 1959 Declaration?

The answer may be found in the 1959 Declaration's Preamble, which states that a child "needs special safeguards and care, including appropriate legal protection, before as well as after birth," which "mankind" owes the child. The 1959 Declaration does articulate children's rights to education as well as protection from exploitation. According to Van Bueren (1998: 9–10), the UN and its member states decided that a separate declaration of children's rights was necessary.

The 1959 UN Declaration formulates a child's social right to education as a claim. Principle 7 of the 1959 Declaration states that: "[t]he child is entitled to receive education, which shall be free and compulsory, at least in the elementary stages." In this same Principle, the Declaration places the responsibility of fulfilling this right on "society and the public authorities [who] shall endeavor to promote the engagement of this right." As such, the 1959 right to education articulates that a young person has a claim to primary education, and society and public authorities have obligations to provide this education.

A social right to health care is articulated in Principle 4. This Principle states that a child "shall be entitled to grow and develop in health"; it also states that a child "shall have the right to adequate nutrition, housing, recreation and medical services." However, unlike the right to education, this Principle does not identify who is responsible for fulfilling this claim. This failure to identify the duty holder confuses the interpreter: the 1959 Declaration does not indicate who is responsible for ensuring young people can exercise rights to health care.

The 1959 Declaration states a civil right to nationality in Principle 3: "The child shall be entitled from his birth to a name and nationality." The right to nationality is supposed to be inalienable. A person should be incapable of relinquishing this right, and an entity, such as government, should not be able to deprive a person of this right. A right to nationality is not a privilege. A person does not have a right to decide whether or not to exercise her right to nationality. The right to nationality is not a claim. While maintaining nationality has costs, we typically do not set up programs or accounts to pay for the right to nationality. Rather, in the case of nationality, a child is granted an immunity according to the 1959 Declaration. Another actor or institution does not possess the ability to alter the child's right to nationality – at least on paper. It is possible that a government actor may try to prevent a young person from exercising her right to nationality, which can lead to dangers in exercising other rights.

Freedom from economic exploitation is an economic right articulated in Principle 9. This Principle states: "The child shall be protected against all forms of neglect, cruelty, and exploitation." Similar to nationality, freedom from economic exploitation is an immunity. This freedom protects young people from another actor or institution trying to exploit them.

While the 1959 Declaration does not articulate children's rights as a bundle, it does specify civil, social, and economic rights belonging to young people. This Declaration does not identify political, participation, and cultural rights of young people. The first declaration of young people's rights since establishment of the UN failed to frame children's rights as a bundle of rights. Given the steps the UN would soon take in regard to human rights, this failure is not a surprise.

International Covenant on Civil and Political Rights and International Covenant on Economic, Social, and Cultural Rights
Adopted in 1966, the International Covenant on Civil and Political Rights (ICCPR) and the International Covenant on Economic, Social and Cultural Rights (ICESCR) entered into force in 1976. Together, the UDHR, the ICCPR and ICESCR are often called the International Bill of Human Rights (United Nations n.d.). The ICCPR and ICESCR are covenants, in contrast to declarations. Following UN adoption, national governments sign, then ratify or accede to the covenant or convention. Upon ratification, a national government is promising to make the covenant's principles and articles its national law. In early 2020, 173 national governments had ratified (or acceded to) the ICCPR, and 170 national governments had ratified (or acceded to) the ICESCR.

The ICCPR and ICESCR enunciate universal human rights, rights that are available to adults and young people. The

ICCPR does not explicitly indicate rights primarily belonging to young people, with a few exceptions. It states that every child has a right to protection as a minor. The ICCPR seeks to ensure that no child is subject to discrimination on the basis of "race, colour, sex, language, religion, national or social origin, property or birth." This same article states a child has the right to acquire a nationality (Article 24, paragraph c). The civil right to nationality is an immunity. The right to nationality is a right that everyone possesses, including young people. This right cannot be taken from, or sold by, an individual.

The ICCPR articulates a freedom of thought, conscience, and religion in Article 18. Article 18 elaborates: "This right shall include freedom to have or to adopt a religion or belief of his choice," as well as how to exhibit this religion. Article 18 clearly enunciates a freedom of religious belief and practice for everyone. As such, this freedom is a privilege available to everyone.

The ICCPR muddies this privilege for young people. Article 18 says that parties to the ICCPR must respect "the liberty of parents" and legal guardians who have the ability to educate their children about religion (Article 18, paragraph 4). This article takes the right to religious belief and practice away from a child. This statement indicates young people are not "everyone," but are instead considered a separate class when it comes to human rights articulated in the ICCPR. By removing this right from a young person and empowering an adult to control the child's religious education, the parent has gained what Hohfeld calls a power. A power gives the right to control an aspect of a person to another individual, including denying a young person a liberty to practice religious beliefs. The ICCPR states that every citizen has a right to vote (Article

25, paragraph b). This article specifies the citizen as the rights holder, not every individual.

Article 6 of the ICCPR prohibits imposition of the death penalty on a person younger than age 18. Articles 22 and 23 forbid marriages that are pre-arranged. The ICCPR establishes an inherent right to life through Article 6, and rights to birth registration and nationality through Article 24. Article 10 states a young person's right not to be jailed with adults. The ICCPR establishes that young people possess a right to rehabilitation following a criminal conviction through Article 14.

Whereas the ICESCR asserts economic, social, and cultural rights that are universally available, this covenant underscores certain children's rights. A social right to compulsory primary education, which is universal, is articulated through ICESCR Article 13. Article 13, paragraph 1 states that national governments that ratify the ICESCR "recognize the right of everyone to education." This statement does not distinguish by any social category, such as age. The Article goes on to assert that "Primary education shall be compulsory and available free to all" (Article 13, paragraph 2a). Secondary education, on the other hand, is to be made generally available and accessible to all (2b), and higher education is to be made accessible to everyone (2c). Article 13, paragraph 2a uses the language of rights when describing the right to primary education. Yet paragraphs 2b and 2c do not use this language. The ICESCR's right to education protects a right to primary education, not a right to secondary or tertiary education. The right to primary education is a claim akin to other rights to education.

The ICESCR's Article 12 articulates the right of everyone to attaining the highest standard of physical and mental health.

Article 12, paragraph 2d elaborates that national governments are responsible for achieving full realization of this right including "creation of conditions which would assure to all medical service and medical attention in the event of sickness." Article 12 uses the language of rights across its paragraphs, but Article 13 does not. The reason for this inconsistency is not clear, but is important when deliberating on what rights young people possess and how to implement them.

The ICESCR does articulate concerns about economic exploitation of young people in Article 10. These concerns, however, are not framed as rights. The Article states: "Children and young persons should be protected from economic and social exploitation," then goes on to say that economic exploitation should be "legally punishable." This Article fails to formulate this protection as a right, including as an immunity. Government or others, such as parents, lack the ability to exploit a young person economically. The person who economically exploits the young person may face legal sanction. The young person, however, does not possess a freedom from economic exploitation.

The UN Convention on the Rights of the Child

As we have seen, adopted in 1989, the UN Convention not only is the most powerful treaty on children's rights, it probably is the most widely ratified human rights treaty. Only the United States, of all UN member states, has failed to ratify the UNCRC. Like the ICCPR and ICESCR, the UNCRC is a convention. Upon ratification or accession, a national government indicates it will make the Convention's provisions part of its national laws and practices. Near-universal ratification suggests that we can reasonably anticipate that the Convention's rights and practices are implemented everywhere.

Child-friendly version of the United Nations Convention on the Rights of the Child, from Save the Children

Article 1
Everyone under 18 has all these rights.

Article 2
You have the right to protection against discrimination. This means that nobody can treat you badly because of your colour, sex or religion, if you speak another language, have a disability, or are rich or poor.

Article 3
All adults should always do what is best for you.

Article 4
You have the right to have your rights made a reality by the government.

Article 5
You have the right to be given guidance by your parents and family.

Article 6
You have the right to life.

Article 7
You have the right to have a name and a nationality.

Article 8
You have the right to an identity.

Article 9
You have the right to live with your parents, unless it is bad for you.

Article 10
If you and your parents are living in separate countries, you have the right to get back together and live in the same place.

Article 11
You should not be kidnapped.

Article 12
You have the right to an opinion and for it to be listened to and taken seriously.

The UNCRC is guided by important principles. Two principles are prominent, which are: ensuring the best interests of the child (Article 3); and non-discrimination (Article 2). These guiding principles mean that national governments that ratify the UNCRC promise to promote what is best for all children. These principles are essential to young people across the world.

According to the UNCRC, a child is someone younger than age 18. The rights to education (Article 28) and health (Article 34) resemble statements in other treaties. A young person enjoys rights to the best attainable standard of health, a Hohfeldian claim. For this right, governments are responsible for its implementation. Article 2(b) says that "States Parties shall pursue full implementation of this right ... and shall take appropriate measures to ensure provision of necessary medical assistance and health care to all children." This Article does assert that governments will strive to ensure no child is deprived of this right (24[2]), then that governments are obligated to cooperate internationally to ensure this right is realized across the world. The UNCRC frames the right to health care as a claim, requiring others to implement the right, as well as an immunity, so that no child will be deprived of health care by another person.

The social right to education emulates the right's articulation in the ICESCR. Article 28, paragraph 1 states a young person has a right to education as a claim. Primary education is compulsory, free, and available to all. Secondary education is to be made available and accessible, eventually developing into being free for all – or, if not free, with financial assistance available. Higher education is to be accessible. The right to education is articulated in the ICESCR and the UNCRC, highlighting its importance as a children's right.

Article 7 restates the ICCPR, which is that a child has the civil right to acquire a nationality. This Article places responsibility for implementing this right on governments' shoulders.

Article 13
You have the right to find out things and say what you think, through making art, speaking and writing, unless it breaks the rights of others.

Article 14
You have the right to think what you like and be whatever religion you want to be, with your parents' guidance.

Article 15
You have the right to be with friends and join or set up clubs, unless this breaks the rights of others.

Article 16
You have the right to a private life. For instance, you can keep a diary that other people are not allowed to see.

Article 17
You have the right to collect information from the media – radios, newspapers, television, etc. – from all around the world. You should also be protected from information that could harm you.

Article 18
You have the right to be brought up by your parents, if possible.

Article 19
You have the right to be protected from being hurt or badly treated.

Article 20
You have the right to special protection and help if you can't live with your parents.

Article 21
You have the right to have the best care for you if you are adopted or fostered or living in care.

Article 22
You have the right to special protection and help if you are a refugee. A refugee is someone who has had to leave their country because it is not safe for them to live there.

Article 23
If you are disabled, either mentally or physically, you have the right to special care and education to help you develop and lead a full life.

Freedom from economic exploitation is an immunity which national governments are responsible for ensuring to a child. Article 32 states that a child is to be protected from economic exploitation, and that national governments shall take legislative, administrative, social, and educational measures.

A child has a privilege of freedom of religion. Like the ICCPR, Article 14 articulates the freedom of religion as a privilege, then goes on to place a limit on this privilege by indicating parents and guardians possess rights to provide direction to the child. This article is distinct from the ICCPR in that the UNCRC states that parents possess the authority to provide direction according to the child's "evolving capacities" (Article 14, paragraph 2).

The UNCRC articulates participation and cultural rights. Article 31 provides that a child should freely participate in cultural life. Article 29 states education should be used to foster a child's cultural identity. However, the UNCRC does not specify a right to vote belonging to young people. Across the major international treaties, described in table 1.2, political rights are glaring omissions when it comes to children's rights. We will return to the UNCRC in chapter 2.

Conclusion

The UNCRC is the contemporary statement of young people's rights. The UN Committee on the Rights of the Child considers the Convention's articles to be aspirations. Some organizations consider the UNCRC to be a baseline. Research indicates that many governments fail to fulfill commitments to children's rights that are articulated in the UNCRC. The same is true of the ICCPR and ICESCR.

When we study roots of children's rights, we see that parents and societies were expected to care for, educate, and prepare

Article 24
You have a right to the best health possible and to medical care and to information that will help you to stay well.

Article 25
You have the right to have your living arrangements checked regularly if you have to be looked after away from home.

Article 26
You have the right to help from the government if you are poor or in need.

Article 27
You have the right to a good enough standard of living. This means you should have food, clothes and a place to live.

Article 28
You have the right to education.

Article 29
You have the right to education which tries to develop your personality and abilities as much as possible and encourages you to respect other people's rights and values and to respect the environment.

Article 30
If you come from a minority group, because of your race, religion or language, you have the right to enjoy your own culture, practise your own religion, and use your own language.

Article 31
You have the right to play and relax by doing things like sports, music and drama.

Article 32
You have the right to protection from work that is bad for your health or education.

Article 33
You have the right to be protected from dangerous drugs.

Article 34
You have the right to be protected from sexual abuse.

young people to contribute to their societies. We would expect that these ideas would be communicated through human rights treaties of the last 100 years. However, a close look suggests children's rights have not been systematically conceptualized. This analysis reveals that a right is articulated as a claim in one treaty, then described as an immunity in a later treaty. Does this discrepancy matter? Yes. A claim requires provision of resources. An immunity merely requires that others refrain from hindering a child's exercise of the right. If a child cannot readily implement the right, an immunity may restrict the child from effectively exercising it. This reliance on immunity may be especially problematic for young people's rights. For many children's rights, young people must turn to adults to exercise their rights effectively. Our analysis suggests that very few of the examined rights are privileges or powers. We can ask why officials of the United Nations and national governments have not extensively established privileges and powers as rights belonging to young people.

We employed Marshall's conception to determine whether young people possess a bundle of rights. The answer is "no." When considering the primary international treaties of children's rights, we note the glaring absence of political rights in the UNCRC, and the conflict with the ICCPR, which states that every citizen possesses the right to vote.

We referred to the UN Committee on the Rights of the Child and the Optional Protocol on a Communications Procedure. As we turn to the next chapter, we may discover that the problems we have identified for children's rights are headaches for institutions working to advance these rights. We may also learn that these dilemmas are part and parcel of how institutions conduct their work on behalf of children's rights.

Article 35
No-one is allowed to kidnap you or sell you.

Article 36
You have the right to protection from any other kind of exploitation.

Article 37
You have the right not to be punished in a cruel or hurtful way.

Article 38
You have a right to protection in times of war. If you are under 15, you should never have to be in an army or take part in a battle.

Article 39
You have the right to help if you have been hurt, neglected, or badly treated.

Article 40
You have the right to help in defending yourself if you are accused of breaking the law.

Article 41
You have the right to any rights in laws in your country or internationally that give you better rights than these.

Article 42
All adults and children should know about this convention. You have a right to learn about your rights and adults should learn about them too.

Articles 43–54 are about how governments and international organizations will work to give children their rights.

CHAPTER 2

Institutions and Children's Rights

Introduction

Now that you are aware that young people possess rights, and have learned about what rights the UN Convention says belong to you and other young people, you must consider how you go about exercising those rights. The Convention is from the United Nations, an important organization about which you already know. Do you contact the United Nations to help you exercise your rights? What organizations will help you exercise rights?

In the previous chapter, we examined the steps leading from formation of the 1924 Geneva Declaration of the Rights of the Child to ratification of the UN Convention on the Rights of the Child. This chapter will take contemporary treaties as its starting point, then examine institutions that have been established to monitor and advance young people's rights (Gran and Aliberti 2003; Thomas, Gran, and Hanson 2011). In this chapter, I will discuss the institutional structures that carry out the work of the UNCRC, and, in turn, describe the UN Committee on the Rights of the Child and its General Comments, independent children's rights institutions, optional protocols, and nonprofit organizations.

At least since the 1924 Declaration, efforts have been made to establish institutions essential to advancing and implementing children's rights (Alston and Tobin 2005). This chapter examines these institutions, the barriers shaping institutions' efforts, and the work they have achieved (Shier 2001). When it comes to human rights, including children's rights, committees hold central positions when monitoring a specific treaty and its national implementations. The UN Committee on the Rights of the Child is the paramount committee tasked with monitoring implementation of the Convention and its optional protocols (Woll 2000). Here we will study the Committee and its work, while trying to assess its impacts on young people's rights and interests. We will devote attention to General Comment no. 2, which calls on nation states to establish national independent human rights institutions that will advocate for and monitor young people's rights.

ICRIs, often known as children's ombudspersons and children's commissioners (Linnarsson and Sedletzki 2014), are considered independent of their government, yet endowed with legal powers to monitor children's rights and act on behalf of young people. ICRIs have not received significant academic attention (but see Lux 2020), yet are believed to play critical roles in the realm of children's rights. The UNICEF study Trond Waage initiated (Linnarsson and Sedletzki 2014) demonstrated that ICRIs are typically charged with monitoring efforts of national governments in implementing the UNCRC, including establishing national legislation that supports children's rights. The present chapter takes a closer look at ICRIs and the work they do in advancing young people's rights.

A third type of institution examined are powerful nonprofit organizations that advocate for and against young people's rights (Cohen 1990). This discussion will consider these organizations' histories, their current membership and funding structures, and how they work to reach their objectives (Seneviratne and Mariam 2011).

Institutions

As the previous chapter suggests, the UNCRC is a basis of an international framework of children's rights. This contention has a basis in a theoretical perspective known as the World Society Approach, which arises from scholarship of John W. Meyer and others.

The World Society Approach has a basis in the new institutionalism perspective. This perspective arises from social science scholarship that seeks to understand how institutions are formed, are maintained, and decline, as well as how institutions establish and impose constraints on actors and organizations (Hirsch and Lounsbury 2015). New institutionalists explore how institutional structures, rules, norms, and pieces of culture constrain and foment choices and actions of people when they are part of an institution (Hallett and Ventresca 2006). Structures of institutions studied by social scientists include membership criteria (Ventresca 2002). Some have concentrated on how rules are organized and used to determine what actions are deemed appropriate and worthy of support, whether in areas of business, nonprofits, government, or legal systems. Other social scientists examine informal rules of organizations, such as the importance of cultural capital in gaining leverage and position (Lareau and Calarco 2012). Sociologists have studied institutional cultures. Sociologists from this perspective view rules, norms, and structures as not necessarily rational or efficient, but perhaps established due to cultural construction (Meyer and Rowan 1991). This perspective, for instance, can look at legal procedures as scripts that institutional members must follow to be considered in good standing (Tremblay and McMorrow 2013).

New institutionalism implies a previous institutionalism,

and, sure enough, there is an old institutionalism. In his article "On the Virtues of the Old Institutionalism," Arthur Stinchcombe provides a big-picture, historical overview of institutionalism. In Stinchcombe's perspective, the old institutionalists were primarily institutional economists not appreciated by other economists, but appreciated by sociologists. These institutional economists prompted Stinchcombe to pursue knowledge of institutions and their roles in the economy. The old institutionalism paid attention to the people who manage institutions. Stinchcombe (1997: 2) says, "Institutionalists were, in the first instance, created by purposive people in legislatures and international unions, and in pamphlets of business ideologists in Northern England." Stinchcombe (1997: 2) seems to emphasize that old institutionalism was more interested in the people who do the creating or constraining of institutions.

The scholarship of John Meyer and others (Boyle 2002; Clark 2010; Cole 2012; Hafner-Burton and Tsutsui 2005; Meyer 1980; Meyer and Rowan 1977; Wotipka and Ramirez 2008) demonstrates that nation states share cultural values and norms when it comes to governing. Together, nation states can establish international frameworks. These frameworks indicate what behaviors are appropriate and how nation states work together in a world society (Cole 2012: 1131; Hafner-Burton and Tsutsui 2005). Human rights are key elements of an international framework of rights (Cole 2005, 2012; Hagan and Levi 2007).

International treaties that articulate human rights are key parts of this international framework (Cole 2012, citing Meyer and Rowan 1977; Boyle and Kim 2009; Hafner-Burton and Tsutsui 2005). Ratifying a treaty and then complying with its rules and procedures may only serve to bolster credibility and maintain appearances. Despite ratification of human rights treaties, societies vary according to whether they implement human rights (Boyle 2002; Boyle and Preves 2000; Boyle and Thompson 2001; Bromley 2014; Deflem and Chicoine 2011; Dobbin et al. 2007; Hathaway 2007; Kim and Boyle 2012; Kim, Boyle, Longhofer, and Brehm 2013; Merry 2006; Savery 2007; Soh 2008). Decoupling is when a national government ratifies a human rights treaty, but does not make the treaty's articles and principles part of its national practice (Cole 2013; Hafner-Burton et al. 2008). Decoupling may occur due to lack of resources (Hathaway 2003) or other "practical considerations" (Meyer and Rowan 1977: 357), or because officials leading the national government never intended to implement the treaties at home (Hafner-Burton 2005).

Surveillance may be used to reduce decoupling. Cole (2012) points out that surveillance may be used to ensure national governments adhere to treaties they have ratified. One surveillance strategy is known as individual complaints procedures. Hafner-Burton and Tsutsui (2007: 421) and Cole (2012) assert that individual complaints procedures may improve human rights practices. Individual complaints procedures may serve to ensure that national governments comply with treaties they have ratified. Below, we take a closer look at the individual complaints procedure of the UN Committee.

The UN Convention on the Rights of the Child

As you know, the UNCRC and its optional protocols are the foundations to the contemporary international framework of children's rights. The UNCRC was adopted and opened for signature on November 20, 1989, then entered into force less than one year later on September 2, 1990 (see figure 2.1). To

Figure 2.1   November 20, 1989 – United Nations, New York. UNICEF holding a press conference as the General Assembly adopts the United Nations Convention on the Rights of the Child. From left to right are: James Grant, Executive Director of UNICEF; Jan Martenson, Under-Secretary-General for Human Rights, and Director, United Nations, Geneva; and Audrey Hepburn, Goodwill Ambassador of UNICEF. (Photo: UN Photo / John Isaac)

become a member party to the UNCRC, governments usually take two steps. The first step is to sign the UNCRC. The signature process consists of a representative of the national government signing the Convention. The second step is to ratify the UNCRC. The ratification process varies by member party. As of 2018, all members of the United Nations have become signatories of the UNCRC. All the UN members but one have ratified: the United States of America is the sole UN member not to ratify the UNCRC.

Despite the reluctance and tardiness of the United States to ratify the UNCRC, US experts shaped the document that ultimately became the Convention (Cohen 2006). One lasting impact of US involvement is the prominence in the UNCRC of the concept of the "best interests of the child." Article 3 (1) of the UNCRC states: "In all actions concerning children, whether undertaken by public or private social welfare institutions, courts of law, administrative authorities or legislative bodies, the best interests of the child shall be a primary consideration." Experts have said that the UNCRC revolves around the best interests of the child. The UN Committee's General Comment no. 14 elaborates on the best interests of the child, which notes that this concept was central to the 1959 Declaration of the Rights of the Child. The restatement of the child's best interests emphasizes its role as a guiding principle (Nauck 1994).

In addition to its Preamble, the UNCRC contains 54 articles. The Convention's Preamble reminds readers of every person's inherent dignity and equality and possession of inalienable rights. Indeed, the Preamble indicates that the UDHR, the ICCPR, and the ICESCR "proclaim" that everyone is entitled to all rights and freedoms, regardless of their skin color, sex, language, religion, or other differences. Why, then, is the UNCRC needed if the UDHR, ICCPR, and ICESCR already indicate that everyone is entitled to human rights? The Preamble reminds readers that the UDHR establishes that "childhood is entitled to special care and assistance," and that a young person should be "afforded the necessary protection and assistance" so she can fulfill her responsibilities to the community and be raised in the spirit of UN ideals. The Preamble also indicates that young people living in vulnerable situations may especially benefit from a UN Convention concentrating on children's rights.

Article 1 identifies what constitutes a child in the eyes of the Convention. By its definition, a child is a person younger than age 18, or younger if the nation state has set a younger age by which a person reaches majority. The UNCRC states principles of how young people should be treated. When it comes to their rights, young people should not experience discrimination and their best interests should be of primary consideration across all society, whether in public or private domains. Rights of young people are supposed to matter wherever the young person is.

The UNCRC seems to build a conflict within the Convention when it points to rights belonging to members of another social institution, the family. The UNCRC articulates the importance of the rights of families, which the Convention's Preamble says is "the fundamental group of society and the natural environment for the growth and well-being of all its members and particularly children." According to the UNCRC, parents hold the primary responsibility for raising a child (Article 18, paragraph 2). The UNCRC also states that working parents have rights to child-care services and facilities (Article 18, paragraph 3). Presumably, these services and facilities must implement young people's rights, including ones to health, nutrition, and security. Article 5 states national governments must respect rights and duties of parents and other family members to provide "appropriate direction and guidance" to the young person when exercising her rights. This conflict is highlighted in the UNCRC in Article 14, which focuses on government respect of a young person's freedom of thought, conscience, and religion. Parents and legal guardians have rights and duties "to provide direction" in the exercise of these freedoms (Article 14, paragraph 2).

However, the Convention does not clearly identify who should offer support to families so that they can meet the best interests of children. The Convention states that, given its fundamental importance, the family "should be afforded the necessary protection and assistance" to fulfill its roles in the community. When it comes to standard of living, the UNCRC indicates national governments must assist parents in ensuring a child's right to an adequate standard of living is implemented, "particularly with regard to nutrition, clothing and housing" (Article 27, paragraph 3). Yet the previous paragraph states that parents have the primary responsibility of ensuring a child's right to an adequate standard of living. It seems, then, that the UNCRC bases the implementation of a child's right to an adequate standard of living on the shoulders of parents and guardians.

The UNCRC articulates rights of young people that we have characterized as civil, political, and social. The Convention asserts that a young person possesses a wide variety of civil rights, including rights to life (Article 6), to name and nationality (Articles 7 and 8), to unification with her family (Articles 9 and 10), to freedom of expression (Articles 12 and 13) and thought and religion (Article 14), and protections from unlawful or arbitrary interference with privacy (Article 16). Young people seem to possess limited political rights, primarily association and assembly (Article 15). (Chapter 3 will concentrate on young people's political rights.) The UNCRC clearly states that young people possess social rights. Young people are entitled to public educations (Article 28), health care (Article 24), and social security (Article 26), among other social rights.

Articles 42 through 54 are written to the UN Committee on the Rights of the Child. The UN Committee holds the responsibility of ensuring national governments that have ratified the UNCRC are implementing those rights at home. These articles identify procedures and principles the Committee is expected to follow.

The UN Committee on the Rights of the Child

The UN Committee on the Rights of the Child is a key component of the international framework established to advance children's rights. Established in 1991, the UN Committee is made up of 18 independent experts who come from countries whose national governments have ratified the UNCRC. While each member is nominated by her home country, she does not represent that country on the Committee. Each Committee member's expenses are paid by the United Nations, bolstering her independence (Alston 1995: 350).

Some features of the UN Committee do raise questions about its independence. Rather than report to all state members, the UN Committee reports to the General Assembly. The General Assembly is responsible for paying expenses of the UN Committee, highlighting at least a potential influence on independence (Alston 1995: 350). It is unclear how much authority the General Assembly has over the Committee. Access of nongovernmental organizations (NGOs) to the UN Committee is through a written submission process (Alston 1995: 369 and n. 202). Interestingly, the UN Committee refers to an NGO as the source of assistance and advice for NGOs that want to report to the UN Committee. The NGO Child Rights Connect has various donors and supporters, including Baker McKenzie, a US law firm criticized for taking a fast-food approach to organizing its practices of law. Another supporter is the Swedish International Development Cooperation Agency (Sida). Sida is a part of the Swedish government that is responsible for implementing the Swedish government's Policy for Global Development (www.childrightsconnect.org/donors-supporters). A "patron" of Child Rights Connect is a former member and Chair of the UN Committee, Swiss Judge Jean Zermatten. These strange relationships between the

UN Committee on the Rights of the Child and Child Rights Connect, an NGO that receives support from a major private law firm as well as the Swedish government, raises concerns about independence of the UN Committee. We can wonder whether these outside groups undermine the independence of Committee members.

Over its existence, the composition of the Committee has changed according to schedule. However, many countries have not enjoyed representation on the UN Committee despite near-universal ratification. Some world regions have enjoyed more frequent representation than other regions. Since 1991, nearly 10 European countries have sent experts to the UN Committee, but over 10 African countries have sent experts. On the other hand, some countries have sent experts more than once. Norway has sent 3 experts, Egypt has sent 4 experts, but the United Kingdom has not sent any.

One of the primary methods by which the Committee promotes children's rights across the world is through requiring national governments to file reports on their work toward implementing the UNCRC. Each national government is obligated to file its first report to the Committee two years after acceding to or ratifying the UNCRC or optional protocol(s). Afterward, the national government is expected to file a report every five years.

After filing its report, representatives of the national government will appear before the Committee. The Committee normally meets three times each year. Its meetings last one month, starting with a presessional working group meeting, followed by a plenary. The presessional meeting is held so that organizations and groups, such as NGOs and children's rights institutions, can provide information to the UN Committee about children's rights in the country concerned. The Committee then shares with national government representatives issues that will be discussed in their meeting. These meetings are open to the public. At the conclusion of the meeting with the Committee and national government representatives, members of the Committee offer a summary of the meeting, along with findings and recommendations. National government representatives can then provide a final statement. Following the meeting, the Committee files Concluding Observations that document a national government's efforts to implement the UNCRC. It is up to the national government to respond to these Concluding Observations, which it will document in its subsequent report. The UN Committee's procedures and norms communicate that children's rights implementation is the responsibility of national governments. It is important to make clear, however, that the Committee can advance children's rights through other means. Concluding Observations are used to "name and shame" a national government through distribution to media (Riley-Smith 2016; Hafner-Burton 2008). The Committee has the power to investigate grave or systematic violations of rights identified in the UNCRC and its optional protocols on child trafficking and children in armed conflicts. We will return to the Committee in chapter 5.

General Comments

The UN Committee publishes General Comments to provide more information on topics of importance to the Committee's work on monitoring the Convention. These General Comments offer elaboration about groups of children, such as adolescents; procedures and policies; and interpreting the work of the Committee. Here we will examine what a General Comment is, criticisms of General Comments, and what may be missing within the General Comments. The General

Comments have articulated rights in new ways. For instance, General Comments nos. 8 and 13 articulate young people's rights to be free from corporal punishment and from violence. While the General Comments articulate these rights as based in old rights, the fact that the UN Committee expresses these freedoms through two new General Comments suggests the perceived need to state these rights explicitly.

The General Comments have articulated new mechanisms for implementing young people's rights. An important example is General Comment no. 2, which imposes on UNCRC member parties the obligation to establish national independent children's rights institutions. As with the new rights, General Comment no. 2 bases this obligation in UNCRC language. However, it is clear that the UNCRC did not explicitly state the expectation that UNCRC member parties would establish independent children's rights institutions as part of their commitments to UNCRC ratification.

The UNCRC has instructed its member parties on how to spend their budgets when it comes to children's rights. General Comment no. 19 (2016, Article 15) indicates that the UNCRC is issuing instructions applicable to budgets of all government branches, at all levels (including provinces and states), and structures. This includes agencies. Indeed, the General Comment's instructions on budget apply to donors and recipients of international cooperation, which presumably includes many international agencies, such as the IMF and World Bank. This step effectively makes children's rights a part of every budget a government entertains, and shapes relationships of different aspects of government, as well as governments' relationships with organizations external to the country.

Most of the General Comments elaborate on rights of distinct groups of young people, such as adolescent young people, children in early childhood, and young people who have disabilities. Some General Comments concentrate on young people in specific situations, such as children living on streets (General Comment no. 21), in juvenile justice systems (no. 10), or who are not accompanied by adults as they migrate (no. 6).

A national government does not accede to or ratify General Comments. However, the Committee does expect national governments to adhere to guidelines published in them. The idea behind this requirement is that a General Comment is merely an elaboration of the Convention. In this way, the General Comments are seen as global structures designed to advance global norms of children's rights. Following this line of thinking, it is important to consider whether a national government is expected to comply with General Comments, given that they are separate from the UNCRC. The UN Committee's rationale of why a national government should treat a General Comment as a legitimate requirement of its efforts to implement the UNCRC is because Article 4 of the Convention states that member parties will "undertake all appropriate legislative, administrative and other measures for the implementation of the rights recognized in the present Convention." Given this perspective, which the UN Committee has reiterated in some General Comments – such as General Comment no. 2 on independent children's rights institutions – commitments of member parties are wide open when it comes to rights articulated in the Convention. As we will discuss, questioning whether these expectations are reasonable is a fair line of inquiry.

As table 2.1 indicates, the Committee does not seem to organize publication of General Comments according to a plan of substantively explaining particular rights or proce-dures around rights. Perhaps one explanation is that the

Committee's composition regularly changes. Another explanation may be that the Committee does publish General Comments in response to concerns that arise. For instance, General Comment no. 8, The Right of the Child to Protection from Corporal Punishment and Other Cruel or Degrading Forms of Punishment, was published in 2006, a time when various components of the UN were working to end violence (see figure 2.2).

In 2017, the Committee published two General Comments on international migration. Both General Comments were co-published with the UN Committee on the Protection of the Rights of All Migrant Workers. It is believed that this pair of General Comments is the first to be built on collaborative work of the UN Committee on Children's Rights and another

Figure 2.2   Children's rights to be free from violence are routinely violated. This photo from 2012 shows a group of young children, all survivors of sexual abuse, being shown at a safe house in Monrovia, Liberia. (Photo: UN Photo / Staton Winter)

UN committee. General Comment no. 22 reasons that the Comment is needed to temper increasing problems international migrant children face and the special vulnerabilities they encounter. General Comment no. 22 asserts that, when it comes to young people, even if a national government has not ratified the UN International Convention on the Protection of the Rights of All Migrant Workers and Members of Their Families, that national government is obligated to protect child migrants because it has ratified the UNCRC. General Comment no. 22 states:

> By virtue of their complementary mandates and shared commitment to strengthening protection of all children in the context of international migration, both Committees decided to develop these joint general comments. While the present comment is based on the provisions of both Conventions, it is important to underline that the human rights norms clarified herein are built on the provisions and principles of the Convention on the Rights of the Child. Therefore, the authoritative guidance contained in the present joint general comment is equally applicable to all States parties to the Convention on the Rights of the Child and/or the International Convention on the Protection of the Rights of All Migrant Workers and Members of Their Families.

This statement makes sense until one considers how many national governments have ratified the Convention on Migrant Workers (CMW). As of 2020, that number is 55, far fewer than for the UNCRC. Indeed, it should be noted that, as of 2020, the CMW has the least number of ratifications of all UN treaties.

The low number of ratifications does not mean children of migrants are not afforded important rights. The CMW reiterates rights other conventions have stated, such as dignity and liberty. Article 17, paragraph 1 of the CMW states:

"Migrant workers and members of their families who are deprived of their liberty shall be treated with humanity and with respect for the inherent dignity of the human person and for their cultural identity." Article 10 of the ICCPR contains a similar provision: "All persons deprived of their liberty shall be treated with humanity and with respect for the inherent dignity of the human person." UNCRC Article 37(c) affirms that "Every child deprived of liberty shall be treated with humanity and respect for the inherent dignity of the human person, and in a manner which takes into account the needs of his or her age." The language of these three articles does not conflict. The ICCPR applies to all people, including migrants and children. The CMW reinforces that migrants possess human rights. The UNCRC merely goes further to insist that a national government must take into account the age of a young person.

The UN Committee does not systematically publish General Comments. Ten years passed before the Committee published its first General Comment. The Committee published three General Comments in 2003, but not one in 2004. The Committee did not publish a General Comment in 2010 or 2012, but published four in 2013. Perhaps a reason for this inconsistent approach to publishing General Comments is that the UN Committee responds to external pressures and changes in Committee composition. Of course, the UN Committee is made up of people with distinct personal experiences and values.

General Comments do deal with many issues (see table 2.1). These issues can concern areas of children's rights, life-course periods, and questions that are not clearly discussed in the Convention. Some General Comments require national governments to establish new sociolegal organizations, such as independent children's rights institutions. As we know, more recently, the UN Committee has worked with other UN committees to publish General Comments on issues that overlap work of both committees.

Table 2.1 General Comments of the UN Committee on the Rights of the Child

General Comment	Number	Date
The Aims of Education: elaborates on right to public education and its importance to other rights belonging to young people.	1	17-Apr-01
The Role of Independent National Human Rights Institutions in the Protection and Promotion of the Rights of the Child: articulates reasons national governments should establish independent human (or children's) rights institutions and what qualities they should possess.	2	15-Nov-02
HIV/AIDS and the Rights of the Child: discusses children's rights in response to HIV/AIDS, to identify and establish positive measures dealing with HIV/AIDS, and developing policies that are child-centric when it comes to HIV/AIDS.	3	17-Mar-03
Adolescent Health and Development in the Context of the Convention on the Rights of the Child: calls on States parties to pay greater attention to adolescents as rights holders while promoting their health and development.	4	21-Jul-03
General Measures of Implementation of the Convention on the Rights of the Child: the UN Committee offers advice on steps States parties should take when implementing the UNCRC.	5	27-Nov-03
Treatment of Unaccompanied and Separated Children Outside Their Country of Origin: this General Comment calls on States parties to consider vulnerabilities and rights of young people who are separated from their families and potentially traveling unaccompanied without their families.	6	1-Sept-05
Implementing Child Rights in Early Childhood: this General Comment both calls upon States parties to give greater attention to early childhood and to bring forth evidence of children's rights during early childhood.	7	20-Sept-06
The Right of the Child to Protection from Corporal Punishment and Other Cruel or Degrading Forms of Punishment: arising from concerns about violence toward children, this General Comment calls on States parties to eliminate corporal punishment of and violence toward young people.	8	21-Aug-06
The Rights of Children with Disabilities: provides recommendations to States parties on implementing rights of children with disabilities.	9	27-Feb-07

Table 2.1 General Comments of the UN Committee on the Rights of the Child (*cont.*)

General Comment	Number	Date
Children's Rights in Juvenile Justice: UN Committee comments on efforts of States parties to implement young people's rights in juvenile justice systems as well as how to help young people avoid entering juvenile justice systems.	10	25-Apr-07
Indigenous Children and Their Rights Under the Convention: this General Comment is prepared to offer advice to States parties on implementing rights of indigenous children.	11	12-Feb-09
The Right of the Child to be Heard: this General Comment is provided to help States parties ensure that young people can express their views and their views receive attention.	12	20-Jul-09
The Right of the Child to Freedom from All Forms of Violence: given alarming levels and instances of violence against young people, the UN Committee publishes this General Comment to call on States parties to prevent violence against young people.	13	18-Apr-11
On the Right of the Child to Have His or Her Best Interests Taken as a Primary Consideration: this General Comment articulates best interests principles and calls on States parties to implement these principles.	14	29-May-13
On the Right of the Child to the Enjoyment of the Highest Attainable Standard of Health: this General Comment contends that children's health should be considered from a children's rights perspective. It reminds States parties that children have rights to survive, grow, and develop considering their well-being across physical, emotional, and social dimensions.	15	17-Apr-13
On State Obligations Regarding the Impact of the Business Sector on Children's Rights: an unusual General Comment, the UN Committee calls on businesses to pay attention to, support, and implement young people's rights.	16	17-Apr-13
On the Right of the Child to Rest, Leisure, Play, Recreational Activities, Cultural Life, and the Arts: this General Comment seeks to articulate rights of young people to recreation, artistic, and cultural activities and calls on States parties to implement these rights.	17	17-Apr-13

Table 2.1 General Comments of the UN Committee on the Rights of the Child (*cont.*)

General Comment	Number	Date
On the Rights of the Child on Harmful Practices (Joint General Comment no. 31 of the Committee on the Elimination of Discrimination Against Women): the UN Committee's first joint General Comment calls upon States parties to give greater attention to violations of rights of women and young women, particularly rights against violence and discrimination.	18	4-Nov-14
On Public Budgeting for the Realization of Children's Rights: this General Comment calls upon States parties to devote public budgets to advancing children's rights.	19	20-Jul-16
On the Implementation of the Rights of the Child During Adolescence: this General Comment calls upon States parties to advance "comprehensive adolescent development" as part of children's rights.	20	6-Dec-16
On Children in Street Situations: this General Comment calls on States parties to establish wide-ranging, holistic approaches to responding to needs and problems young people face while living without homes "in street situations."	21	20-Jun-17
Context of International Migration: General Principles: the first joint General Comment with the UN Committee on the Protection of the Rights of All Migrant Workers and Members of Their Families calls upon States parties to pay attention to and implement rights of young people who are migrants.	22	16-Nov-17
States' Parties' Obligations in Respect to Countries of Transit and Migration: this General Comment identifies responsibilities of States parties in implementing and advancing rights of young people who are migrants.	23	16-Nov-17
On Children's Rights in the Child Justice System: this General Comment replaces General Comment no. 10. It calls on States parties to consider contemporary principles around child justice systems and to implement children's rights in those systems.	24	18-Sept-19

Is it fair and reasonable to expect national governments to implement requirements and expectations the UN Committee articulates in its General Comments? The UN Committee views the General Comments as part of the UN structure of advancing rights. National governments that have ratified the UNCRC are expected to comply with the General Comments, thereby expanding their obligations as part of an international framework of children's rights. Is that a fair assumption for national governments? To answer this question, let's consider independent children's rights institutions, the subject of the UN Committee's General Comment no. 2.

Independent children's rights institutions

The UN Committee's second General Comment indicates the Committee's expectation that national governments will establish independent children's rights institutions (ICRIs). We discussed the concern that national governments and others may interpret requirements articulated in General Comments as beyond rules and expectations dictated by the Convention. This General Comment on ICRIs was adopted 13 years after UNCRC adoption (UN Comm. Rights Child 2002, paragraph 1).

To be clear, ICRIs have not been established in every country whose national government has ratified the UNCRC. In some countries, ICRIs are called children's ombudspersons or children's commissioners (Gran 2011; Gran and Aliberti 2003). Despite publication of the General Comment, objectives, structures, legal powers, and independence of ICRIs do vary (Gran 2011). ICRIs based in European countries concentrate on whether their national governments are implementing the UNCRC and enforcing rights of young people (Gran and Aliberti 2003). ICRIs have been established in the United States, but these ICRIs are not concerned with rights of all young people. Instead, their focuses are constrained to young people in state care or in the criminal justice system. A question we can ask is why US ICRIs work to protect and monitor rights of young people who spend time inside juvenile detention centers and state care systems (Gran 2020).

ICRIs may be endowed with legal powers. Children's ombudspersons and commissioners can use these powers to advance children's rights (Gran 2011). The first Children's Commissioner of England investigated a detention center holding young immigrants to whom the state was failing to provide education and other services (Launer 2009). Independence, however, is crucial to an ICRI exercising its powers. Initially, the English Commissioner was required to consult with the Secretary of State before conducting a public inquiry. While taking controversial positions, the Norwegian Office of the Children's Ombudsperson has experienced pressures on its independence (Samuelsen 2011). Government demands can undermine an ICRI's legitimacy. ICRIs are increasingly found across the world. On paper, ICRIs are powerful offices that can advocate for young people and their rights. Many ICRIs have the responsibility of advocating to their national governments for the advancement of global norms of children's rights. In practice, legal arrangements, limited resources, restrictions on independence, and other factors constrain the work of children's ombudspersons and commissioners in protecting and promoting children's rights. It seems that some national governments establish ICRIs without wanting those offices to pursue children's rights.

Optional protocols

Because the UNCRC cannot be amended, what happens if we want to incorporate a new right into the Convention?

One strategy the UN Committee has taken is to adopt optional protocols. Three optional protocols to the UNCRC have been adopted. The first is the Optional Protocol to the Convention on the Rights of the Child on the Sale of Children, Child Prostitution and Child Pornography (OPSC). Since its adoption in 2000, as of early 2020, 176 national governments have ratified this optional protocol, including the United States. A second optional protocol to the UNCRC is the Optional Protocol to the Convention on the Rights of the Child on the Involvement of Children in Armed Conflict (OPAC), which was also adopted in 2000. As of early 2020, 170 national governments have ratified this optional protocol, including the United States. This optional protocol is significant because it prohibits people younger than age 18 from military service, as well as illegal compulsion of young people into participating in military hostilities.

These two optional protocols highlight an interesting fact regarding the United States. The US national government is the only UN member not to have ratified the UNCRC, yet it has ratified two of the three optional protocols to the UNCRC. How could the United States take this approach of ratifying two optional protocols, but not the Convention itself? The answer is that the optional protocols are distinct. The US national government has agreed to incorporate articles of the optional protocols into national law, yet is unwilling to take this step when it comes to principles and laws of the UN Convention. This approach suggests US residents have mixed feelings around the UN and children's rights. Conversely, some national governments that have ratified the UNCRC have yet to ratify the optional protocols.

The third optional protocol to the UNCRC is the Optional Protocol to the Convention on the Rights of the Child on a Communications Procedure. Through this optional protocol, the UN Committee is permitted to hear individual cases. As of early 2020, only 46 national governments have ratified this optional protocol, which was adopted in 2011. The US national government has neither signed nor ratified this optional protocol, and probably will not move forward until it ratifies the UNCRC.

It remains unclear what impacts this optional protocol will have on children's rights (Hafner-Burton and Tsutsui 2007: 421). One reason is that the UN Committee can only consider a child's complaint if that child's national government has ratified the optional protocol. A second reason is that the UN Committee's power to respond to the child's complaint is limited. The UN Committee can only make a recommendation to the child's national government that it respond and remedy the violation of the child's right. The individual complaint procedure does not endow the UN Committee with powers to remedy the rights violation. Instead, the UN Committee depends on the national government to enforce the child's right.

Nonprofit organizations

Powerful nonprofit organizations are part of the international framework of children's rights. Some of these organizations advocate for, and some advocate against, young people's rights (Cohen 1990). What are these organizations? How do they work toward their objectives (Seneviratne and Mariam 2011)? Where do they fit in this framework?

In the previous chapter, we discussed the work of an organization that became Save the Children. Today, Save the Children is among the most powerful nonprofit organizations that advocate for children's rights. Save the Children undertakes work in specific countries that seek to promote the interests of young people and advance their welfare.

This organization also advocates for the well-being of young people at national and international levels. Save the Children raises funds across the world, then deploys those funds in over 128 countries.

As a nonprofit organization invested in advancing all rights of all children, Save the Children has few peers. International nonprofit organizations that advocate for human rights, such as Human Rights Watch and Amnesty International, do work on behalf of young people's rights, but these efforts are among broader efforts to promote human rights. Two newcomers are the "Hope for Children" CRC Policy Center and KidsRights International. Taking the UNCRC and other international laws that support young people's rights as its guiding documentation, "Hope for Children" works with academics and policy makers to advance children's rights in general. Similarly, KidsRights calls attention to young people's rights through various efforts, including an annual award called the International Children's Peace Prize.

Some nonprofit organizations concentrate on particular rights of young people, while others take an international approach or concentrate on domestic efforts. The Global Initiative to End Corporal Punishment seeks to end physical punishment of young people (End Corporal Punishment 2020). Its strategies include working with governments to pass laws and establish structures to prevent corporal punishment, and advocating to national and international organizations for its abolition. In the United States, the Collaborative to End Human Trafficking has concentrated its efforts on human trafficking in the state of Ohio. The Collaborative uses a three-pronged approach that consists of education, advocacy, and networking of service providers. The Collaborative leadership has led workshops and trainings in law enforcement agencies, hospitals, universities, and schools so that people can learn about human trafficking and how to prevent it. Collaborative leadership has lobbied members of the Ohio state legislature, as well as federal officials. Finally, Collaborative leadership has sought to transform a hodge-podge of service providers into a strong safety net of services for trafficking victims. In many societies, young people would face significant hurdles and holes in social service and welfare state nets without the efforts of nonprofit organizations.

Nonprofit organizations are essential actors that help ensure young people experience implementation of their rights, as well as advancement of their interests and welfare. While international nonprofit organizations play significant roles that supplement other efforts, national and local nonprofit organizations are key to ensuring young people enjoy their rights, and that their communities support those rights.

Conclusion

An institutional approach to studying organizations reveals a framework of organizations that not only advance children's rights, but also foster norms and expectations and provide rules and procedures around securing young people's rights. This approach also helps us discover holes and weaknesses in this framework of children's rights.

In the following chapter, we will concentrate on young people's political rights. The right to assemble and right to vote will be a focal point in this inquiry. We will discover that, while the UNCRC articulates a right to assemble, it does not indicate that young people possess the right to vote. Consequently, the UN Committee has not asked UNCRC member parties to promote young people's right to vote. We will see variation in voting ages across countries and analyze the reasoning behind these differences. Upon reading chapter

3, it is vital that we come to understand that this institutional framework of children's rights includes holes that can lead to failures in enforcement and advancement of young people's rights.

Children's Political Rights

Introduction

Now that you are aware that you possess rights and what institutions are useful to exercising these rights, you wonder which rights are available to you. You notice signs calling on you to vote for a candidate in an upcoming election. On the way to school, you notice billboards asking for your support of a political party. You wonder how elections work and how you can join a political party.

You soon discover that you are not eligible to vote and you cannot become a member of a political party. You inquire about forming a political party, but are told that a young person cannot start her own party. Rather than doors opening, you are discovering that voting and joining or starting a political party are not open to you.

Societies, to varying degrees, are organized so that some people and some groups possess more power than others. Doors only open to members of some groups. Resources are only available to members of some groups. Political sociologists are often interested in how power works and who possesses it. They study how people use political power to exert authority to either produce or prevent social change. Political sociologists want to understand why and how members of some social groups are excluded from decision making and the organizations through which power is exerted.

Political rights make up one category of rights that is part of the bundle of rights that T. H. Marshall (1950) identified as essential to being a full member of society. As you know, in his *Citizenship and Social Class*, Marshall offers a vision of citizenship that consists of a bundle of three kinds of rights: civil, political, and social. Political rights are tools to bring about political change, which can be used to bring about transformations in other rights and society in general. According to Marshall, the possession of political rights is an indicator that an individual is a societal member. We will see, however, that young people's possession of political rights is limited in many ways. This lack of possession raises fundamental questions not only for young people's bundle of rights, but also for their societal membership. Exclusion from political rights indicates individuals are considered ineligible, and perhaps inadequate, to participate in decision making through established organizations.

In this chapter, we will touch upon what defines politics, and examine the politics surrounding children's rights. We will then explore statuses of young people's political rights around the world, and what political rights may potentially do for young people.

What is politics?

Politics has been the subject of intellectual attention and debate from the start of humankind. Definitions of politics are many, but the majority share qualities that are important to political rights. For example, Aristotle said politics are used to govern society (Aristotle 1994 [350 BCE; Lord 1984]). Correspondingly, Foucault said politics are used to exert power (Foucault 1975). Lay people can use politics to exert power over political leaders. Political leaders can use politics to exert power over lay people, which can bolster or thwart lay people's effective exertion of power over political leaders (Arendt 1951). Politics can be used to identify who is a member and who is not a member of society (Benhabib 2000). Politics can be used to protect and prevent disadvantage from bearing down on them (Esping-Andersen 1990).

Despite these broad understandings of politics, young people have fallen outside the purview of these definitions. In his idea of the state, Aristotle does give attention to young people, but young people are outside politics in his conception. They are subject to the rule of their parents. When the parents improperly rule their children, then male citizens can step in to rectify the situation. As we have discussed, however, powerful questions have been raised about whether the state will intervene into the family home and other private domains.

On the other hand, Foucault does extend politics to children. However, Foucault's analysis concentrates on the family. He contends that discipline has been extended into the family: "absorbed by the family" (Taylor 2012: 202). This discipline is extended through education, medicine, and other institutions. This discipline is external to the family; the social institutions are outside the family, yet their influence and power shape the internal functioning of the family and its relationships. Foucault contends that parents turn their children over to a disciplinary institution when they send their children to school. This institution, a school, returns the children as disciplined and prepared to participate in their families, communities, and societies according to expectations (Taylor 2012: 204–5).

According to Foucault, however, as they raise their children, ensure they receive medical and dental check-ups, and make certain they attend school, parents continue to hold power over their children. This kind of power relationship is due to blood; societies treat biological parents as special holders of power over their children. Foucault indicates that a biological father holds the most power: "What do we see in the family if not a function of maximum individualization on the side of the person who exercises power, that is to say, on the father's side?" (Foucault 2003/6: 80, cited Taylor 2012: 204). Of course, this understanding of biological fathers intersects with Aristotle's notion of the state and the roles of male citizens as fathers. Aristotle and Foucault seem to suggest that a young person is subject to the rule and power of her parents. Can political rights modify this one-sided relationship?

What are political rights?

What are political rights? In previous chapters, we have spent time getting to know T. H. Marshall's (1950) work on citizenship and citizenship rights. To Marshall, citizenship consisted of a bundle of three kinds of rights: civil, political, and social. For Marshall (1950: 14), political rights started with rights of "franchise" and "qualifications for membership of Parliament." In his telling, Marshall (1950: 19) explains that political rights existed, but were "distribution-defective." What Marshall (1950: 19) intends to communicate is that political rights existed, but did not meet the standards of democratic citizenship. What Marshall means is that only some members possessed political rights. Political rights include rights to assemble and to vote (see figure 3.1 Janoski 1998: 30–2). Many potential members of a democracy did not possess political rights. Marshall goes on to point out that, while most people (his estimate is 20% of the British adult male population could vote) could not employ political rights, an important change was under way that recognized people possess the *capacity* to exercise political rights (1950:

19–20). "No sane and law-abiding citizen was debarred by personal status from acquiring and recording a vote" (1950: 20). To Marshall, British society was moving toward ensuring all adult citizens possessed political rights. He does not reflect on political rights of noncitizens.

Experiences of noncitizens, such as migrants, can shed light on statuses of young people. Soysal (1994) points out that many countries prohibit noncitizens from participating in national elections: "National voting rights for aliens are, in fact, very rare" (1994: 127). She finds that "local voting rights," the ability to vote in a non-national election such as at the local and regional levels, has been extended to noncitizens in some

Figure 3.1   The school strikes for climate, initiated by Greta Thunberg in August 2018, are one example of children mobilizing their capacity to exercise political rights, by assembling together and asking for change. (Photo: Brisbane School Strike / Flickr)

countries (1994: 127–8). In some countries, noncitizens can vote and stand for office in both local and regional elections. Despite these opportunities, Soysal concludes that the primary way for noncitizens to participate politically is *indirectly*. Soysal (1994: 154) contends that the question of political participation, for a migrant compared to a "national citizen," "cannot be divorced" from the fundamental distinction that the migrant is not a citizen. Referring to claims by migrants of voting rights, Soysal categorizes suffrage not only as a participatory right, but as an essential aspect of human personhood (1994: 154). Children are treated like noncitizens when it comes to their political rights. Across most societies, young people do not possess the right to vote. Instead, their political interests are assumed to be implemented indirectly through their parents' exercise of political rights. We count on parents to exercise their political rights in ways that ensure the best interests of their children are advanced.

Politics of children's rights

Politics of children's rights play out throughout all societies. Even in societies where children's rights are not discussed, or are even *avoided*, that is saying something about the rights of young people. Here, we approach our study of politics and children's rights through an analysis of organizations in which politics play out.

Politics of children's rights play out at all levels of society, including international, national, regional, and local levels. At the international level, of course, the focus is on the UNCRC and its Committee. The truth is that young people's rights play out across other international organizations, nonprofit organizations, and in other ways at the international level.

At the international level, over 25 UN organizations have the potential to influence rights of young people. Politics are part of these organizations, but we must question whether organizations' politics affect young people's rights. Are children's rights part of the work conducted by those organizations' employees and leaders? Do the rights of young people have a place on their agendas?

The answer to this question is, for the most part, "no." To examine politics of children's rights in these international or regional organizations, a useful approach is to compare these organizations by type. Scholars have grouped international organizations according to three categories: purpose, membership, and structure (Miles 1968). Purpose defines whether or not their purpose is general or specific. This category identifies the concentration of objectives explored by a given organization. In other words, it notes whether an organization's work encompasses multiple objectives or concentrates on one objective, such as health care. Membership is the degree to which member states belong to the organization. For example, this category outlines an organization's universality or its limitation to member states of a particular region. On the other hand, structure clarifies whether or not the organization has a formal structure based in a constitution or treaty agreement. For the purposes of this analysis, we will concentrate on international organizations that have structures based in formal agreements. Consequently, we will compare organizations according to membership and purpose, two features that illuminate whether young people's rights and interests are key concerns of the individual organizations (see table 3.1).

Let's start with the United Nations (UN). Founded in 1945, the UN consists of 193 member states. According to the UN Charter, the UN's mission is to maintain international peace and security, and promote international relations and cooperation that can be used to solve international problems. In spite of human rights being among its chief concerns, the UN does

Table 3.1 Types of international organization		
Membership	Universal	Limited
Purpose		
General	United Nations	Organization of American States
Specific	World Bank	African Committee of Experts on the Rights and Welfare of the Child

not have an office focused on children's rights. Instead, the UN Children's Fund (formerly known as the United Nations International Children's Emergency Fund [UNICEF], but still commonly referred to as UNICEF), concentrates on children's rights and is guided by the UNCRC. UNICEF works in 192 countries. While UNICEF concentrates on young people's well-being, education, gender equality, and inclusion, it does not focus on young people's political rights. It excludes, for example, children's right to assemble and right to vote. However, UNICEF's "participation resource guide" does offer research papers detailing how to bolster young people's societal participation. Some of these papers concentrate on young people's political rights. For instance, the participation resource guide includes a paper produced by the Children's Rights Alliance for England that calls for enabling people of ages 16 and 17 to vote (United Nations Children's Fund 2006). Nevertheless, UNICEF does not appear to have established a focus or taskforce that concentrates on advocating for political rights of young people. Including a focus on young people's political rights could provide momentum to establishing more widely children's rights to vote.

An international organization whose membership is universal but whose focus is specific is the World Bank. The World Bank is a powerful organization whose mission is two-fold: (1) end extreme poverty; and (2) "promote shared prosperity." The World Bank does not act as a site of politics regarding young people and their rights – at least not directly. Children's rights are politicized at the World Bank not through routine measures, but instead as issue measures. That is, the World Bank does not host sustained efforts to advance young people's rights – which exclude their political rights. Instead, the World Bank deals with young people's rights when they arise as issues. The World Bank lacks an office or position, such as an ombudsperson, that routinely monitors children's rights in the context of its work and efforts.

One issue to which the World Bank has devoted time and resources is stunting. Stunting is lack of, or slow, physical development of a young person, and is part of the UN's Sustainable Development Goal #2 on Hunger. UNICEF, the WHO, and the World Bank have developed a joint project on stunting that is part of the Joint Child Malnutrition Estimates, where the World Bank and UNICEF gather, record, and publicly share information about the stunting of young people across countries. This project focuses on the Sustainable Development Goals (United Nations Children's Fund, WHO, and World Bank n.d.). This work does not concentrate on young people's rights, ultimately excluding their political rights. Through its relationship with UNICEF, the World Bank takes an issues-approach to advancing children's rights. The failure to collaborate on young people's political rights is a lost opportunity.

The World Bank has been challenged for its apparent disregard of human rights. Philip Alston (2015), the United Nations Special Rapporteur on extreme poverty and human rights, has openly criticized the World Bank for its failure to incorporate human rights in its work. Alston's efforts do not come as a surprise; he is a tireless advocate and scholar of human rights who seems to be taking advantage of the independence of the UN Special Rapporteur role. Professor

Alston's challenges can arguably be extended to young people's rights.

An international organization whose membership is limited but whose purpose is general is the Organization of American States (OAS). Established in 1948, the OAS's mission is organized around four pillars: democracy, security, development, and human rights. The central mission of the OAS does not include children and their rights – it has not set up an office that monitors the work of the OAS in consideration of advancing young people's rights. Its membership consists of 35 individuals. While human rights is one of its pillars, the OAS has established a distinct organization that routinely concentrates on young people's interests, including their rights. This separate organization, the Inter-American Children's Institute, indicates that the OAS treats young people and their rights as distinct from humans and their rights. Given its focus, the Children's Institute may be a smart strategy for advancing children's political rights.

The Inter-American Children's Institute was established almost 20 years before the OAS, but became part of the OAS in 1948. A mission of the Institute is to assist member states in advancing young people's rights, including rights articulated in the UNCRC. Despite the UNCRC omitting a young person's right to vote, the Institute has undertaken research on young people's political rights. In 2007, the OAS Inter-American Children's Institute published the article "Políticas públicas y derechos humanos del niño" (translated as "Public Politics and the Human Rights of the Child"). Despite the implication of a strong political rights focus suggested by the title of this work, political rights are not part of the Institute's 2015–19 Action Plan. The Action Plan does include the item of increasing participation of young people, such as giving voice to young people. The Action Plan does not tackle a young person's right to vote. In sum, while the Institute does routinely address children's rights, these rights do not include political rights of young people. As its name suggests, the OAS is concerned with people living in the western hemisphere. Other regional organizations have been established to promote young people's rights.

The African Committee of Experts on the Rights and Welfare of the Child has a limited membership whose purpose is specific and focuses on children's rights. The African Charter on Rights and Welfare of the Child was adopted in 1990 and entered into force in 1999. Currently, the Charter has over 50 member states. It resembles the UNCRC in many ways, including in its articulation of the rights of assembly, and a failure to state a young person's right to vote. As of September 2020, the Charter has been signed but not ratified by 5 member states, including the Democratic Republic of Congo, Sahrawi Arab Democratic Republic, Somalia, South Sudan, and Tunisia. One state has neither signed nor ratified, which is Morocco. The African Charter does not seem to enjoy universal support among African countries.

The African Committee of Experts on the Rights and Welfare of the Child consists of 11 independent experts whose terms last 5 years. Currently, professional backgrounds of the Committee members include social work, law, psychology, and medicine. The experts' home countries are countries that are Charter members. The Committee holds ordinary sessions twice each year. It can hold extraordinary sessions either upon the Committee's decision or in response to a written request from a Charter member. An ordinary session mirrors a UNCRC Committee session. While initial reports are expected 2 years after ratification, periodic reports are expected every 3 years. In addition, the Committee publishes General Comments. The topics of these General Comments

range from "child marriage" to incarcerated parents to responsibilities of children. This latter General Comment, published
in 2017, does not identify a responsibility of a young person
to exercise political rights.

The African Committee does take stands in regard to the
Charter's member states. In 2009, the Committee published
a decision in response to a complaint filed by the Institute
for Human Rights and Development in Africa and the Open
Society Justice Initiative on behalf of Children of Nubian
Descent in Kenya, against the government of Kenya. This
complaint requested that the Kenyan government provide
Kenyan nationality to Nubian parents and children, which
had been denied through failures of Kenyan legal processes.
Ultimately, the Committee *recommended* to the Kenyan
government that it provide nationality to the individuals
whose interests were articulated in the complaint. As of 2017,
the Kenyan government had not followed through on recommendations of the African Committee. While this is but one
example, it suggests that the African Committee possesses
limited authority when it comes to young people's rights.
Consequently, we may question whether the African Charter
is useful in protecting and promoting children's rights.

Politics of young people's rights are relegated to specialized
institutions. Perhaps this relegation to specialized institutions arises from a common perception of young people as a
special social group whose interests and rights require special
attention. However, this perception seems to belie the fact
that young people, their interests, and their rights tend to
remain outside the central domains, debates, and concerns
of universal organizations whose purposes are general and
specific. Unless these specialized institutions can powerfully
assert the interests of young people, their efforts to advance

young people's rights will probably be, at best, slow and perhaps ineffective.

Children's political rights

A glaring omission in human rights of young people is the right to vote (Wall and Dar 2011). The UNCRC makes no provision for young people possessing and exercising the right to vote. While this omission might seem sensible on the surface level, it must be challenged. This challenge has the potential to demonstrate that the failure to guarantee the right to vote to young people is a grave error on the part of both the UNCRC and the Committee.

T. H. Marshall does seem to suggest that political rights can produce significant social change that people holding authority and power may fear. Consider the following:

> The political rights of citizenship, unlike the civil rights, were full of potential danger to the Capitalist system, although those who were cautiously extending them down the social scale probably did not realise quite how great the danger was. They could hardly be expected to foresee what vast changes could be brought about by the peaceful use of political power, without a violent and bloody revolution. (1950: 25)

This quote suggests that perhaps those individuals who oppose children's rights fear peaceful use of political power and the potential meanings young people give to their rights. In some societies, we find organizations whose purposes include giving young people experience with political rights. Youth Parliaments are typically established to provide experiences with rights to assembly and vote (see figure 3.2). Some

Youth Parliaments are empowered to propose a bill to the (adult) Parliament. These Youth Parliaments effectively deploy peaceful power in advocating for young people and their rights.

Youth Parliaments

Youth Parliaments empower young people to exercise their political rights in two ways: through assembly and through voting. Youth Parliaments are organizations through which young people assemble, make decisions about the societies in which they live, and convey those decisions to the (adult) Parliaments (see table 3.2). We find Youth Parliaments in Europe, Asia, Africa, Oceania, and the Americas. Most Youth Parliaments meet once each year, allowing their Members to exercise their rights to assemble annually.

Figure 3.2 A session of the East Africa Youth Parliament in 2019. (Photo: WFD.org)

Table 3.2 Locations of Youth Parliaments

Africa	Americas	Asia	Europe	Oceania
African Youth Parliament	Youth Parliament of the Americas	India	European Youth Parliament	National Indigenous Youth Parliament of Australia
Tunisia	Argentina	Timor Leste	Albania	YMCA Youth Parliament of Australia
	Canada (British Columbia, Quebec)		Armenia	New Zealand
	Chile		Austria	
	Jamaica		Azerbaijan	
	Mexico		Belarus	
	Peru		Belgium: Dutch	
			Belgium: French	
			Bosnia and Herzegovina	
			Croatia	
			Cyprus	
			Czech Republic	
			Denmark	
			Estonia	
			Finland	
			France	
			Georgia	
			Germany	
			Greece	
			Iceland	
			Ireland	
			Italy	
			Latvia	
			Lithuania	
			Luxembourg	
			The Netherlands	
			Norway	
			Poland	
			Portugal	
			Romania	
			Russia	
			Scotland	
			Serbia	
			Slovakia	
			Slovenia	
			Spain	
			Sweden	
			Switzerland	
			Turkey	
			Ukraine	
			UK	

A mission common to Youth Parliaments is to encourage young people to involve themselves in their nation state's political processes. This mission is oriented to assisting a young person in becoming an effective user of their adult rights. In some instances, young people exercise their voting rights through electing Members of Youth Parliaments.

When an individual becomes a Member of a Youth Parliament, she exercises her right to vote. For the most part, Members of Youth Parliaments are limited to using their votes to shape the affairs of the Youth Parliament. Some Youth Parliaments are empowered to propose a law that the (adult) Parliament will consider and possibly pass. While this vote does not carry the same weight as an adult Parliamentarian's vote, the vote of a Youth Parliamentarian demonstrates that young people can and do act thoughtfully and peacefully.

Figure 3.3   A young representative addresses the East Africa Youth Parliament, 2019. (Photo: WFD.org)

Youth Parliaments demonstrate the value of implementing young people's political rights.

Let's take a look at three Youth Parliaments to gain a better understanding of how they function. In Australia, the first Youth Parliament was held by the YMCA in 1963. According to the Victoria YMCA, over 100 young people spent two weeks together collaborating to give a presentation to the Queensland Parliament's Legislative Council. In 1985, 22 years later, the Victoria YMCA's State Director proposed to a group of young people living in Victoria the establishment of a Youth Parliament. Over 30 years ago, in 1987, Victoria's Youth Parliament met for the first time in the Victoria Parliament's Legislative Council.

For the Victoria YMCA, young people who participate go to a nine-day training program. This training program is residential, meaning that the young people live together as they train. The program concludes with the Youth Parliamentarians holding debates in the Victoria Parliament over three days. The focus of these debates, the Victoria YMCA reports, are issues of concern to young people. The Victoria YMCA is an example of how young people can assemble to discuss and exercise their political rights effectively.

The Timor Leste Youth Parliament, Parlamento Foinsa'e Nian, was established in 2009. The mission of the Timor Leste Youth Parliament is not to implement young people's political rights. Rather, its mission is to encourage young people to become involved in Timor Leste's political processes. Its membership includes people aged 12 to 17; 2 Parliamentarians represent their home subdistricts for a total of 132 Parliamentarians. Rather than being elected by their peers, candidates are instead selected at the subdistrict level. For the Timor Leste Youth Parliament's future, Timor Leste's Secretary of State for Youth and Sport is expected to approve a statute that will create a two-stage election process. The first stage will allow candidates to campaign in their subdistrict's schools and meet students in those schools. In the second stage, candidates will "face a test in front of a board of examiners." While the first stage empowers other young people to exercise their political right to elect a Parliamentarian to represent them, the second stage potentially thwarts these political rights.

Members of the Timor Leste Youth Parliament make recommendations to the National Parliament and the Secretary of State for Youth and Sports. In addition, Youth Parliamentarians discuss issues with government officials, as well as lead campaigns and initiatives about issues of importance to young people. Timor Leste Youth Parliamentarians have represented the country to national and international conferences in Australia, Indonesia, and Spain. Parliamentarians are supposed to participate in national discussions, as well as raise concerns about issues affecting young people living in their subdistricts. Local government officials are expected to brief Parliamentarians on Timor Leste issues. UNICEF and the Timor Leste Secretary of State for Youth and Sports support the Timor Leste Youth Parliament.

The United Kingdom Youth Parliament (UKYP) takes a similar approach to Timor Leste. UKYP consists of over 600 members. Elections of UKYP members, though, are determined by the district in which the young person lives. Some districts employ a "first past the post" approach, for instance. Similarly, some Members are selected by voluntary organizations in Scotland.

This overview of Youth Parliaments suggests that these organizations are important means by which young people can exercise political rights. If a young person's right to assemble is exercised through assembling to vote, then the

Youth Parliament's meeting and work also implement a young person's right to assemble. A young person's right to vote is exercised through voting in elections for Members of the Youth Parliament.

Right to Vote

Earlier in this chapter, we noted that a young person's right to vote, a key political right, is not articulated in the UNCRC. The age at which young people may legally vote varies across countries. The age of 16 is the lowest for any country's national elections. In some countries, young people can vote at ages younger than 16 for sub-national elections. Here we will explore those voting ages, then deliberate on rationales offered for setting voting ages.

We first note that voting is compulsory in some countries. In 21 countries, governments mandate that individuals must vote (see table 3.3). In these countries, a person who fails to vote may pay a fine. Among countries where voting is compulsory, only 2 governments mandate that people younger than age 18 are required to vote. Greece and North Korea have established universal and compulsory voting for people who are age 17 and older.

In contrast, people of ages 16 and 17 may voluntarily vote in national elections of 5 countries. Those countries include Argentina (16), Ecuador (16), Sudan (17), and Timor Leste (17). In some countries, people of age 17 can vote in municipal elections, but not until age 18 in national elections. Estonia, Germany, and Israel are among these countries.

If they meet particular legal conditions, people can vote at ages 16 and 17 in Hungary, Serbia, and Slovenia. In Hungary, while the voting age is set at age 18, if a person is married, and the marriage is registered, she can vote at age 16. In Serbia and Slovenia, one can vote at age 16 if one has a job. Voting is not

Table 3.3 Countries where voting is compulsory for national elections	
Country	Voting age
Argentina	18 (16–17 can vote voluntarily)
Australia	18
Belgium	18
Bolivia	18
Brazil	18 (16–17 can vote voluntarily)
Costa Rica	18
Democratic Republic of the Congo	18
Dominican Republic	18
Ecuador	18 (16–17 can vote voluntarily)
Egypt	18
Greece	17
Honduras	18
Luxembourg	18
Mexico	18
Nauru	20
North Korea	17
Paraguay	18
Peru	18
Singapore	21
Thailand	18
Uruguay	18

compulsory in Serbia or Slovenia. Vote16USA is an advocacy organization in the United States that calls for lowering official voting ages to 16 years. Their efforts are focusing on the states of Colorado, Hawaii, Illinois, Maryland, Massachusetts, and the cities and towns of Berkeley, California; Brattleboro, Vermont; Culver City, California; Hyattsville, Maryland; San Francisco, California; and Takoma Park, Maryland; as well as Washington, DC.

This analysis of voting ages reveals that many political leaders and voters do not want to extend suffrage to people who are younger than age 18. Most countries have set the age at which a person can vote in a national election to age 18. Why are people who are younger than age 18 denied the right to vote? In what follows, we will examine the justification of competency (Wall 2014), as well as the possible answer of ageism.

Competency means capacity or ability to act. The *Oxford Dictionary* defines competency as the ability to do something successfully or efficiently. *Black's Law Dictionary* defines competency as being "Duly qualified; answering all requirements; adequate; suitable; sufficient; capable; legally fit." These definitions share qualities of ability to act or refrain from acting in socially appropriate ways. Across jurisdictions, competency can be a key component of legal actions, including providing consent to medical procedures, entering into marriage, registering for military service, and being held criminally responsible. For centuries, thinkers like Socrates have asked whether competency is necessary to exercising political rights.

A striking finding demonstrated in table 3.4 is that age by which competency is set not only differs across countries, but also by type of competency within each country. For many of the countries examined, the youngest ages at which a person is considered competent is in relation to the commitment of crimes. For example, a person as young as 7 or 8 can be held criminally responsible. Only one country, Brazil, sets an age of criminal responsibility higher than the age at which an individual can vote in national elections. On the other hand, the age at which a young person can join the military service without parental consent tends to match voting ages across a handful of examined countries, including Paraguay, Slovenia, the United Kingdom, and the United States. Another group of countries set the minimum age at which a person can serve in the military higher

Table 3.4 Age of competency and voting age, various countries					
	Medical consent	Enter marriage (male female)	Military service without parental consent	Criminally responsible	Voting age
Argentina		18 18	21	16	16
Austria	Depends on child	16 18	18	14	16
Brazil		16 16	17	18	16
Cameroon		18 15	18	10	20
Ecuador		14 12	18	12	16
Germany	Depends on child	16 16	17	14	18
Indonesia		19 16	18	8	17
Malaysia		18 16	17.5	10	21
Paraguay		14 14	18	14	18
Slovenia	15	15 15	18	14	18
UK	16	16 16	18	10	18
United States	Depends on state	14 12 (dependent on state)	18	7	18

than the age at which a person can vote in a national election. This group includes Argentina, Austria, Brazil, Ecuador, and Indonesia. Only Cameroon, Germany, and Malaysia set older ages for voting in comparison to military service.

For most of the selected countries, the age at which a person can enter into a marriage is lower than or equal to the age at which a person can vote, for example in Brazil, Cameroon, Ecuador, Germany, Malaysia, Paraguay, Slovenia, the United Kingdom, and the United States. The governments of Argentina, Austria, and Indonesia take different approaches. Argentina prohibits marriage until the parties reach age 18, while the voting age in Argentina is 16. In Austria, a male can marry at age 16, but a female cannot marry until reaching age 18. Similarly, the national voting age of Austria is 16. Indonesia takes a different tack. A male cannot marry until reaching age 19, but a female can marry at age 16. Indonesia's national voting age is 17.

This analysis suggests that competency probably is not a sensible rationale supporting voting ages across countries. In the examined countries, ages at which persons can register for military service or enter into a marriage or be held criminally responsible vary. It is also important to note that no country has set the age of competency for entering into these different social relationships to the same level as the national voting age.

If not competency, then what explains established national voting ages? One explanation is that national governments design and implement inconsistent frameworks around competency. As a rule, policy analysts want to assume government leaders understand procedures and consequences when it comes to designing and implementing laws. It is possible that the design of the laws surrounding competencies of marriage, military service, criminal responsibility, and voting is undertaken with weak logical bases that are not informed by medical and scientific research. That is to say that government leaders may not incorporate expertise when establishing standards and rules on competency.

Without precluding this possibility, another explanation may be ageism. Governments may discriminate on the basis of age against younger people. Governments appear to make haphazard decisions when it comes to setting age to areas of competency. For nearly all examined countries, the lawful age at which a person is held criminally responsible is younger than the age at which a person can vote in national elections, with the exception of Argentina (same age) and Brazil (older age). The difference in ages between criminal responsibility and national voting ranges from 11 years (in Malaysia and the United States) to 2 years (in Austria).

Turning to consider the UNCRC bolsters this conclusion that ageism is a strong explanation for why voting ages are set high. The UNCRC, *the* Children's Rights Convention, does not articulate a right to vote for young people. This omission is most likely intentional. The right to vote is stated in Article 21, paragraph 3 of the Universal Declaration of Human Rights and Article 25(b) of the International Covenant on Civil and Political Rights. If the right to vote is a universal human right, its lack of availability to people younger than age 18 (or 16 or 17) suggests that young people are experiencing age-based discrimination. It is ironic that the UNCRC incorporates ageism into its principles and rules.

Conclusion

Politics about children's rights are not discussed in organizations with universal membership and general purposes. As Alston (1995) contends, this failure to address young people's rights in these large organizations that significantly influence world events and the ways in which we live may be intentional. Instead, politics about children's rights are either routine matters of organizations whose purposes are specific, or matters of organizations that collaborate to tackle particular issues. Failures of large, international organizations to take children's rights seriously in their own work and their collaborations with other international organizations are a loss to children across the world.

Youth Parliaments represent opportunities for young people to exercise their rights to vote and to assemble. However, in the big picture, often these organizations do not have the same impacts as people exercising their rights to vote and assemble when it comes to (adult) Parliaments. The unwillingness to allow young people to exercise their political rights through Parliamentary elections and actions is disheartening. Certainly, these are missed opportunities.

These dubious restrictions are not surprising given the apparent ageism toward political rights. Despite the ability to charge young people with crimes, the unwillingness to allow young people to vote – and, in some places, people of older ages to vote, as suggested by our analysis – indicates that political leaders and voters struggle to decide what to think of young people and their rights.

In the next chapter, we will examine meanings children give to their rights. We will learn that many young people discern impacts of their rights, as well as why their rights matter to society. These meanings provide insights into what we may achieve through children's rights.

CHAPTER 4

Meanings of Children's Rights

Introduction

Children's rights are articulated in international treaties, such as the UNCRC, and through national laws (Waibel 2014). Yet whether and how those rights matter to young people are unclear. Here we will study how young people think about their rights. One question on which we will deliberate is why we do not know more about what children think about their rights.

To a young person – and, for that matter, anyone – a right may convey different ideas and offer important meanings. Exercising a right may empower a young person to open the doors to an institution that offers resources and opportunities (Osler and Osler 2002). Through enjoying her freedom of conscience, a young person may think and act independently (Langlaude 2007). Correspondingly, a "bundle of rights" (Marshall 1950) may empower a young person to change relationships and circumstances that are part of being a member of society.Possessing a right may mean to a young person that they are a member of a community (McCluskey, Riddell, and Weedon 2015).

Yet a right may have little meaning to a young person. Young people may be unaware of rights they possess on paper. A young person may conclude that rights are not relevant to the life they live. This young person may not possess resources she needs to exercise rights (Archard 2014a). She may reach a conclusion that rights do not belong to her, but to members of other social groups (Balagopalan 2014). Institutions needed to exercise rights may be out of reach to young people, or perhaps be organized so that rights fail young people (Chunli 2006). A right may be ineffective to a young person whose crucial needs are not met. A young person may grow up in a community whose culture opposes the idea of rights (Boyle and Preves 2000). Young people may understand rights as impositions that are contrary to their experiences, wants, and needs (Pupavac 2011).

This chapter reviews what we know about the meanings young people ascribe to rights, their implementation, and barriers they encounter in trying to exercise those rights. It provides information about studies that reveal that many young people are aware of their rights and how they may use them. This chapter will also demonstrate that, despite these valuable studies, we need to learn more about the meanings young people ascribe to their rights.

How can we learn about what rights mean to young people?

An advantage sociologists enjoy, of course, is that we can ask people what they think. There are multiple ways to learn what young people think about their rights. Social scientists employ a wide variety of approaches to learning about what people think or believe, and how they perceive their experiences. You are likely aware of methods that incorporate surveys, focus groups, and interviews. Each approach offers advantages to gathering information about young people's experiences with, and opinions of, their rights. We will examine how these approaches have been employed to study young people's rights.

Sociologists often employ surveys. There is a good chance you have participated in a survey. A survey seeks to gain information from a sample of individuals who are members of a population. A survey typically asks questions of its participants (Fink 2013). These questions can ask for all kinds of information, from the participant's experience to their perspective and opinion, to demographic information, such as age. Sociologists employ many forms of surveys, including Internet-based surveys and in-person surveys. Sociologists use surveys because they are versatile, efficient, and generalizable (Schutt 2018). Surveys are versatile because they can ask a host of questions, and are efficient because surveys can be administered to many people at the same time. If the researcher aspires to generalize her findings from survey participants to the broader population, she can follow professional practices to make generalizations.

Perhaps you have participated in a focus group. A focus group is an interview, but an interview of a group of individuals. The leader of the focus group poses questions to the group of participants. An advantage of a focus group is that participants can respond to each other while answering questions the leader asks (Ochieng, Wilson, Derrick, and Mukherjee 2018). Another advantage is that focus groups support opportunities to consider deeply questions the leader poses to the group of participants. Focus groups can be efficient, but rarely can a researcher generalize from a small group of participants.

You may have been interviewed. Many approaches to interview are available to sociologists. A common strategy is to ask open-ended questions – that is, questions without prescribed answers. This approach of asking open-ended questions enables the participant to give answers that come to her mind, rather than responding to choices the interviewer offers. An interview can enable the sociologist to learn about feelings, experiences, and opinions of the participant. While an interview can help a sociologist gain deep understanding, interviews are time intensive. As a result, most sociologists cannot undertake a sufficient number of interviews to make generalizations based on the participants involved.

Global studies of young people's opinions and experiences do not exist, but cross-national and national studies do. Researchers have not employed the same instrument to ascertain young people's opinions in every country. As we will see, cross-national and national studies have been undertaken, but only of young people living in a handful of countries. We will review what those studies say, draw connections across the studies to identify patterns and differences in what young people think about their rights, and then consider what else we want to know. While outstanding studies have been undertaken to learn what young people think about their rights, more information is needed.

But why do we want to know what young people think? A key aspect of young people's rights is whether and how young people exercise their rights. A treaty or a constitution may articulate rights, but an individual may not be aware of those rights or may not believe that he or she can exercise them. If an individual cannot or does not exercise rights when those rights may help, we should wonder and ask why.

What do social science studies say about young people's experiences with their rights?

Here we seek to identify patterns in young people's experiences with, and opinions of, their rights. Our strategy is to review studies other researchers have undertaken. We try to draw conclusions from these studies, bearing in mind limitations of our approach. As mentioned, global studies of young people's opinions and understandings of their rights are not available. What are available are studies undertaken at regional levels, comparisons of individuals living in two countries, and within-country studies. Some studies concentrate on particular aspects of young people's understandings and experiences with rights. Other studies focus on offices charged with implementing young people's rights. These studies reveal what young people think about their rights, and whether these offices are doing good jobs in supporting young people's knowledge and exercise of their rights.

Awareness of Rights

A question we may first ask is whether young people are aware that they possess rights. Answers to this question, of course, are key to what young people think about their rights, organizations needed for exercising their rights, and what young people think should happen once their rights are implemented.

It turns out that *where* a young person lives seems to shape their awareness that they possess rights. The same is true of *when* young people are queried about awareness that they possess rights. One of the most extensive studies of what and how young people think of their rights was undertaken for the European Union by Dr. Antonis Papacostas, head of the Eurobarometer Unit. For the 2009 study, Flash Eurobarometer 273, Dr. Papacostas (2009) surveyed young people between the ages of 15 and 18 who live in 27 European countries: Austria, Belgium, Bulgaria, Cyprus, the Czech Republic, Denmark, Estonia, Finland, France, Germany, Greece, Hungary, Ireland, Italy, Latvia, Lithuania, Luxembourg, Malta, the Netherlands, Poland, Portugal, Romania, Slovakia, Slovenia, Spain, Sweden, and the United Kingdom. Dr. Papacostas undertook a similar study, Flash Eurobarometer 235, in 2008. Across the same

27 European countries, for 2009, 66% of the Eurobarometer sample indicated their awareness of young people possessing rights over the course of one year. The 2008 study found 67% of young people indicated awareness of young people possessing rights. This stable result indicates a large proportion of European young people are aware they possess rights.

A comparison of opinions and experiences of young people living in Spain and Italy sheds light on young people's perceptions of their rights. This study administered a questionnaire to young people living in the Catalan region of Spain and the Molise region of Italy (the authors of this study refer to the Molise region as Il Molise). The study asked whether children possess rights, and what a right is. Nearly 89% of the Spanish Catalan participants, and over 94% of the Italian Molise participants, indicated they know what a right is. In both the Catalan and Molise samples, a higher proportion of young women answered affirmatively, compared to young men. Over 91% of Molise women participants answered affirmatively, compared to 86.7% of the young men. The difference between young women – 76.6% – and young men – 60.9% – who responded affirmatively in the Catalan sample is striking.

Are Young People's Rights Protected?

A question we may ask is whether young people believe their rights are protected. As you know, children's rights are inalienable (Children's Rights Alliance for England 2018). Children's rights cannot be taken away from them and they should not be violated. In Dr. Papacostas's 2009 study of 15- to 18-year-olds living in 27 European countries, when participants were asked how well rights of young people in the participant's country are protected, about 14% of the participants said they were very well protected, and about 64% said fairly well protected. This means a lower proportion believe rights are well protected, but a higher proportion indicate they are fairly well protected. On the other hand, about 2% said they were not protected, and 20% said they were not very well protected. That means about 78% indicate young people's rights are protected in their countries, but 22% indicate those rights are not well protected, or worse. The 2008 study produced similar results. About 16% of the participants said rights were very well protected, and about 60% said fairly well protected. On the other hand, about 3% said they were not protected and 20% said they were not very well protected. Thus, while 76% acknowledge protection of young people's rights, 23% indicate those rights are not well protected. This set of findings suggests that, while young people may recognize they possess rights, they are concerned whether their rights are protected from violations. Although treaties and laws may assert that children's rights cannot be violated or taken away, many young people express concerns that their rights are not protected. This perception – that rights are not protected – may weaken commitments to treaties and laws articulating human rights and young people's rights.

What Rights Do Young People Think They Possess?

What rights do young people believe they possess? We now recognize that not all young people believe they possess rights, and that many children believe their rights are not protected. In their comparative study of young people living in the Catalan region of Spain and Molise in Italy, researchers asked participants to identify rights that belong to young people. While this section of the researchers' report is difficult to follow, rights to education and school receive most attention, with over 40% of the Catalan and over 30% of Molise participants indicating that young people possess these rights.

Some young people value basic needs over rights to leisure and recreation. The next most common right to receive attention differed between Spanish and Italian participants. For the Catalan sample, over 21% pointed to a right to meet basic needs. In contrast, 12.4% of the Molise sample pointed to this right. On the other hand, about 31% of the Molise sample pointed to rights surrounding leisure and recreation, to which only 10.6% of the Catalan sample gave attention. The researchers do not provide systematic explanations of these differences. Their study is significant and expecting them to do so is unfair. We can wonder, however, if differences are due to cultural experiences participants have in both geographic areas. These differences may arise because young people witness socio-economic deprivation, recognize the value and importance of rest and recreation, their educations may incorporate materials that give attention to issues surrounding these areas of rights, and so on. A bottom line, however, is that these differences exist and are important. Across the world, young people's experiences and opinions with their rights can vary. This sociological phenomenon, that experiences with rights are not necessarily uniform or produce expected outcomes, demonstrates the value and importance of asking young people what they think in general, and about their rights in particular.

The researchers asked a question at the intersection of the right to education and disability. They offered a scenario to seek opinions as to whether young people support the right to public education. Asking whether or not a girl who is blind has the right to attend a school with children who can see, nearly 76% of the Catalan sample and over 66% of the Molise sample supported this girl's right to attend the same school. This finding suggests that many young people – but not all – desire equal rights to education for everyone. Another question about education the researchers posed to participants intersects with economic rights. The researchers asked participants whether they consider it fair for a young person to miss school if they have to work for the family business. As the researchers note, this question is meant to ask young people about their perspectives on rights to welfare protection, as well as to freedom from economic exploitation. Large, comparable proportions of participants in both samples deemed this situation inequitable. Over 89% of the Catalan and over 90% of the Molise sample indicated this situation is unfair. The researchers asked about the right to associate. They asked young people whether they considered it fair if children could only participate in a social activity as part of the village festival if parents participated. Over 50% of participants in both samples indicated this situation was unjust.

A focus group is a methodological approach that can reveal young people's opinions and perspectives on their rights. In a study of rights and citizenship among New Zealanders, researchers undertook studies of eight focus groups of young people (Taylor, Smith, and Gollop 2008). The study's participants consisted of two age groups, two socio-economic groups, and people who live in urban or rural areas. Of the focus groups' 66 participants, 32 were between the ages of 8 and 9, and 34 were ages 14 or 15. Of these participants, 34 self-described as of "low" socio-economic status and 32 as "high" socio-economic status; 39 were from urban areas and 27 were from rural areas. Directors of the focus groups successfully organized group participants to vary across social categories expected to be important to experiences with rights.

How did this study "work?" The researchers met with members of each focus group, first providing an explanation of the study, then asking the participants to complete a consent form. The researchers' next step was an exercise through which participants shared their names and in what cities they were born, which facilitated a discussion of what it means to be a member of the New Zealand community. Then the researchers asked participants to write down their rights, then picture their lives in an imaginary country. This step was designed to enable participants to separate themselves from their lives in New Zealand to imagine what they ideally want.

Participants categorized rights across types, then across domains: participation, provision, or protection rights in the home, school, and community (Lansdown 1994). Participants articulated participation rights as "having a say" in the home, school, and community. Participation rights at home included independence. At school, participants wanted to influence decision making through mechanisms like student councils. In the community, participation rights included rights to movement, and control over one's time and space. Participants articulated provision rights as fulfilling tangible and intangible needs. At home, participants identified needs of shelter, clothing, kindness and love, as well as money, such as an allowance, and entertainment. At school, participants wanted opportunities to learn, to access teachers and learning materials, and to study in environments conducive to learning. In the community, participants identified opportunities to obtain health care, access safe recreation, and work and earn money. The list of protection rights at home is much shorter and is the right to be safe at home, free from violence. The participants do not seem concerned with external threats; instead, they are concerned with threats within the home. Also, protection rights at school include the right to be safe, as well as the administration's need to take seriously bullying and its prevention. Protection rights in the community extend concerns about bullying and personal safety. Participants also discuss non-discrimination as a protection right.

The researchers employed the interesting innovation of asking participants about their lives in an imaginary country. This approach empowers participants to think beyond their circumstances of living and growing up in New Zealand. The researchers report key rights that the participants raised. Rights to safety were raised, such as prohibiting violence against young people and restrictions on weapons. Another set of rights revolved around health and well-being, as well as access to leisure and recreation. The researchers note that access to education was the most commonly identified right, but that participants called for making school interesting and enjoying more choices when it came to school.

For this part of the focus group, living in an imaginary country, the researchers classified one right as respect and participation. Older participants noted the importance of rights to be listened to and to have representation. Younger participants indicated similar rights, as well as having their ideas presented to government. The right to vote was raised, as well. The researchers asked whether young citizens living in the imaginary country should have more rights than they do in New Zealand. Nearly all responded in the affirmative.

A focus group enables a small gathering of individuals – people who typically do not know each other before the focus group starts – to share ideas and experiences. A focus group allows these individuals to reach consensus as well as disagree on issues. This approach may stimulate further thinking on questions. These New Zealand researchers took advantage of these advantages of focus groups to learn more about meanings young people give to their rights. Their use of an imaginary country empowered participants to think beyond their own experiences to consider what they ideally want when it comes to young people's rights.

Competing Rights

As we know, sometimes the rights of two people can compete. We know very little about how people make decisions between rights, especially when those rights belong to young people. While judges, lawmakers, and policy makers often have to make such decisions, young people are rarely asked what decisions they will make when it comes to competing rights. We do not know whether young people's perceptions will differ, and, if so, differ according to different social groups.

The Catalan and Molise study asked participants to make decisions between competing rights. To study perceptions of privacy, the researchers presented a scenario of a parent opening a letter addressed to their child from one of their child's friends. Over 49% of the Catalan sample indicated they would be upset, and over 47% of the Molise sample indicated they would be upset. The researchers find differences by gender. In the Catalan sample, a higher proportion of girls than boys regard this situation as a privacy violation, while in the Molise sample a higher proportion of boys than girls consider this situation to be troubling. This difference is revealing for many reasons, and the researchers should be applauded. One revelation is that differences in views of children's rights can vary by country, even if those countries' national governments have ratified the UNCRC. Likewise, another revelation is that differences in views of children's rights can vary by social group, such as gender and age. In addition to providing new insights, this study reveals that differences in perspectives of competing rights can differ according to gender and age. This set of findings suggests sociologists and other social scientists should investigate differences per social groups and experiences.

Some studies present scenarios about children's rights. The Catalan and Molise study asked their participants about the nature of children's rights. One question asked participants to choose whether to exclude a girl from participating in a school play because of her language abilities, or whether the group of performers should proceed with the play while including the girl. A small fraction of the participants chose to exclude the girl. When asked why, the participants who recommended inclusion said the right to participation was more important than a group feeling satisfied with their theatrical work. This result confirms the finding that, despite ratification of the UNCRC, views of children's rights can vary by country. As above, views of children's rights can differ by social group – for instance, according to gender and age.

Variations in perspectives may depend on the right being considered. The UNCRC articulates rights to family. The Eurobarometer study asked about a situation in which parents are divorced, and one parent moves to another European Union member state, so that "a new decision on the children's custody and access rights has to be taken," to which nearly 72% responded it was the right thing to do. This result suggests that young people believe government has a role in changing custody situations that affect young people.

This finding is bolstered by the study of young people living in Spain and Italy. Researchers find high proportions of Catalan participants and Molise participants believe young people should have the right to indicate their preferences for living with a particular parent when their parents split up. Nearly 83% of the Spanish and 84% of the Italian samples believe young people possess a right to indicate this preference. Given high proportions of marital dissolution and challenges to custody decisions, this finding reveals that young people have a stake in decisions around their custody. They believe they possess a right to express their opinion about custody decisions.

Problems with Exercising Rights
Through the Flash Eurobarometer studies he directed, Dr. Papacostas inquired into problems a young person might

Table 4.1 Problems young people experience when trying to exercise rights (Papacostas 2008, 2009)

What are the problems you think people under 18 years of age might encounter when they need help to defend their rights?	% mentioning this problem (2009)	% mentioning this problem (2008)
Not aware of rights	80.5	79.5
The procedures are too complicated	71.9	70.8
They do not know how to go about it and whom to contact	81.3	81.5
The authorities (public administrations such as, for instance, city councils, ombudsman) do not respond	56.5	56.5
Another reason	77	74.1

experience when needing help in defending her rights. The Eurobarometer study indicates that across 27 European countries, young people identify significant problems for children trying to exercise their rights (see table 4.1).

An interesting surprise is that, across two domains of the two Flash Eurobarometer studies, a larger percentage of participants mention these problems in the later study. In 2009, a higher proportion of young people are not aware of their rights. In 2009, a higher proportion of young people state that procedures around children's rights are too complicated. We cannot ascertain reasons for these increases, but their increase over time, particularly the problem of young people not being aware of their rights, is a concern. Why would fewer young people be aware of their rights later in time?

In addition to being unaware of their rights, over 80% of participants believe young people do not know how to exercise their rights and whom to ask for help in exercising their rights. A significant hurdle seems to be that young people consider procedures to be too complicated. Bearing in mind that survey participants are young people between the ages of 15 and 18, these findings suggest significant hurdles must be overcome to ensure that rights are useful to young people.

A finding that is not surprising yet reveals a disconnect between rights on paper and rights in practice is demonstrated when taking a closer look at those who seek help with rights violations. From this same study, less than 5% of participants themselves sought help with an issue when they thought their own rights were violated. Over 10% of participants said that they knew of someone who sought help with an issue when they thought their rights were violated. This result suggests a disconnect. On the one hand, 81.5% indicate not knowing whom to contact or what steps to take to seek help with a matter involving their rights. On the other hand, approximately 95% indicate they did not seek help with an issue when they thought their own rights were violated. This difference of 13% is problematic for the use of young people's rights. This finding indicates that 13% of the respondents, people between the ages of 15 and 18 in 27 European countries, did not pursue guidance or assistance in exercising their rights, even when they knew whom to ask for help in exercising those rights. Perhaps this result indicates some young people do not view their rights as useful. This view may arise from mistrust of government or the legal system.

One sign that this problem is possible to overcome is that about 25% less of the respondents indicate that government authorities, such as public administrators and ombudspersons, do not respond to problems young people experience when needing help with their rights. That is, a lower proportion of participants indicate a view that young people have problems with government officials in seeking help exercising their rights. While 56.5% is high, this proportion is much lower than the proportion of those surveyed who believe young people do not know how to exercise their rights and whom to ask for help in exercising their rights. Government officials, especially human rights and children's rights ombudspersons, can do more to help young people exercise their rights. One step forward may be raising the profiles of these offices so that more young people are aware of what they do and can do on behalf of young people. Of course, a critical step is establishing an office of the children's ombudsperson in places where young people live. Independent children's rights institutions are key organizations to disseminating information about rights to children.

The right to information is key to many rights and arises from the right to education. In a study of young people's right to information, researchers (Kennedy and Covell 2009) conducted a survey of 120 Canadian high school students (their median age was 15.4 years old). The kinds of information on which the researchers focused surrounded sex and sexuality (Langille, Andreou, Beazley, and Delaney 1998). The students were enrolled in two high schools in the province of Nova Scotia in Canada. The researchers were able to obtain a sample that was representative of Nova Scotia. Caucasian participants made up 94.5% of the study, 3.6% were African Canadian, and 1.8% were "other." The researchers asked participants to self-identify. Of the 120 students, 63 students were male and 52 were female. To be clear, the researchers asked participants about their experiences and opinions of sexual health education, sexual health knowledge, as well as sexual activity and sexual prejudice.

Based on results of the survey they administered, the researchers found sexual health knowledge among the participants was, in general, poor. The researchers drew the conclusion that their survey findings reveal that sexual health education is not consistent with children's rights to information. These researchers point out that a valuable resource on sexual health knowledge was available but denied to students. Their study revealed sexual prejudice in schools. The researchers are careful to scope their findings to experiences in schools and indicate that sexual prejudice is not limited to schools. As a consequence, students not only are denied information and knowledge that affect their sexual health, but also their right to information in school. This denial of a young person's right to education, the researchers argue, weakens a child's best interests. Based on findings from the survey they administered to students enrolled in two Nova Scotia high schools, Kennedy and Covell (2009) conclude that violations of the right to information, especially around rights to health and bodily control, do not fulfill young people's best interests, a key principle of the UNCRC.

Perceptions of children's rights: the roles of children's ombudspersons

A study of the Office of the Children's Commissioner for Wales provided insights into how young people think of children's ombudspersons or commissioners regarding their rights (Hillman, Taylor, Pearson et al. 2010). A children's ombudsperson is similar to a children's commissioner. Sometimes distinctions are in name alone, but a commissioner is expected to advocate while an ombudsperson is expected to act on a complaint (see Gran 2011). While the Welsh study did not strictly concentrate on young people's rights, participants did answer questions about their rights over the course of the study. The research team, associated with the University of Central Lancashire, consisted of Thomas, Cook, Cook, France, Hillman, Jenkins, Pearson, Pugh-Dungey, Sawyers, Taylor, and Crowley. They planned the study and recruited young people as researchers from networks of youth in southern Wales. The younger researchers were between ages 12 and 20, and numbered 15 at the start of the 3-year study. By the study's conclusion, 10 young people were contributing to the study. This study undertook a school-based survey as well as stakeholder interviews. The study aimed to achieve triangulation. Thomas and colleagues pursue triangulation by employing two research methods, the survey and interviews, to check the reliability and validity of their study's evidence.

Because the research team wanted to study awareness of the Office of the Children's Commissioner and the work of the Commissioner, the team administered a survey of students aged 7 to 16 years old. The research team worked with local education authorities to identify potential participants. To reach objectives of assessing awareness of the Commissioner's office and work, the research team asked young people about their rights. The team repeated the surveys over two academic years, 2006–7 and 2007–8, thereby allowing the team to obtain samples of two groups of students. For the 2006–7 year, 62 sets of surveys were returned, leading to 1,373 completed surveys. For 2007–8, the team returned the sets of surveys to the same 62 classes, from which 53 sets were returned, leading to 1,155 completed surveys.

This team asked participants about their recognition of the Welsh Office of the Children's Commissioner. Their study revealed low levels of recognition. Only around 5% of participants recognized the brand of the Welsh Office of the Children's Commissioner. On the other hand, around 60% of participants indicated that young people possess rights in both waves of the survey. About 30% of participants were aware of the UNCRC, with most indicating they were aware of the UNCRC via the Internet and TV. Participants mentioned a host of rights when asked what rights children have, including food and water, warmth and shelter, being safe and looked after, staying healthy, education, free speech, freedom and equality, and play. These results may reveal that although young people may not be aware of the Welsh Children's Commissioner, they are aware of the work of the Commissioner, and the work of the Commissioner is advancing children's rights.

I enjoyed a visit to the Office of the Children's Ombudsman of Iceland (see figure 4.1). During my stay, I accompanied the Ombudsman (the office is called 'Ombudsman' – this ombudsman was a woman) and an anthropologist, a member of her office, during a visit to an elementary school. Their visit was designed to raise awareness of children's rights among the students. The anthropologist had employed his education, training, and experiences to develop an educational program appropriate to elementary students. He had organized this program to be implemented in a classroom of young, active students. Our visit took place in the morning, at the start of

Figure 4.1   A snapshot of a team working with and for children's human rights: the staff of Iceland's Children's Ombudsman (left to right, Auður Kristín Árnadóttir, Margrét María Sigurðardóttir (Ombudsman), Eðvald Einar Stefánsson, and Elísabet Gísladóttir)

the school day. Upon arrival, a school administrator escorted us to a room that was two classrooms whose dividing wall was retracted allowing for two groups of students to participate in the visit. As the Ombudsman and anthropologist set up their presentation, I took a look around the classroom, examining desks, books, and classroom materials. Next to the door of the classroom, I noticed that a child-friendly summary of the UNCRC was posted. Perhaps this document had been posted right before our visit, but the document seemed to have been there for a while. From what I could see, information about children's rights is distributed in Iceland's public schools.

The Ombudsman started the visit by greeting the students and introducing her colleague and herself. She asked the students to raise their hands if they had heard of the UNCRC; nearly all hands went up. The Ombudsman spoke only a minute more, then the anthropologist explained the group activities they were going to try. One activity was a game in which students worked together to decide what essential possessions they would need if they were alone, without adults present. Some students concentrated on shelter, some on clothing, some on food, some on communication devices. The Ombudsman and anthropologist incorporated the students' needs into a discussion of the young people's rights. After the visit, the anthropologist explained how he had constructed the activities, referring to research about how students learn, and how Iceland school culture is taken into account. The activities and conversations kept the students' attention. The visit, although less than an hour in length, had clearly made an impact on the students. They paid attention to the presentations, then were engaged in the activities. Before leaving, the Ombudsman explained how students could find her office geographically and electronically, and that she welcomed any conversation with all young people. This visit and its activities were powerful tools to share information with young people about their rights, the work of the Children's Ombudsman, and how the young people could contact the Ombudsman's Office.

This visit provided many insights into how people, especially young people, can learn about children's rights. It seems to me that the activities of Iceland's Children's Ombudsman are employed by other children's ombudspersons. There are smart, effective ways of promoting children's rights. These means are time consuming, but effective, and one component of the ombudsperson's work. In addition to disseminating information about children's rights to young people, members of the Ombudsman's Office analyzed Iceland's legislation, monitored enforcement and implementation of children's rights, and collaborated with Icelandic government offices and nonprofit organizations.

It seems that young people's awareness of their rights requires actions and contributions by multiple actors, whose efforts together advance children's rights. Another factor to consider is culture. The anthropologist and Ombudsman explained that Icelandic socio-political culture supported young people's rights. While there were ongoing concerns about the rights of immigrant children, overall the Ombudsman and anthropologist believe Iceland's people supported children's rights. This support, of course, makes the work of the Office of Iceland's Children's Ombudsman easier.

Fair questions to ask are: (1) is Iceland especially open to human rights?; and (2) does Iceland's society enjoy a culture that is supportive of children's rights? These questions are difficult to answer concretely. I have not been able to identify an international measure of cultural resistance to children's rights or human rights, for that matter. Indices of human and children's rights are available, but these indices do not consider cultural resistance to children's rights. Scholarship on such cultural resistance tends to focus on cases of individual countries, or comparisons of small numbers of countries. These studies demonstrate that cultural resistance can play a big part in whether and how children's rights are implemented. Nevertheless, drawing comparisons across the world is not currently possible.

What should be done when it comes to young people's rights?

Because of their experiences and because they pay attention, young people have opinions and perspectives on what efforts should be undertaken to promote their rights. Let's return to the Flash Eurobarometer studies Dr. Papacostas directed. Offering five choices, the Flash Eurobarometer study asked 15- to 18-year-olds living in 27 European countries what steps young people consider to be high priorities at the European level to promote and protect young people's rights. Table 4.2 presents those five choices, and what proportion of 15- to 18-year-old participants indicated each action as a high priority.

Bearing in mind that participants responded to the choices they were offered, over 93% gave high priority to providing more information to young people about their rights and where to inquire about them. Responding to this priority does not require extensions of the legal system. To tackle this issue, national governments and NGOs need to provide more information and new strategies to disseminate information to young people about their rights and how to inquire about them. What does that entail? Government officials, ombudspersons, and NGO representatives can visit schools, post information on school transportation, and establish Youth Parliaments.

Table 4.2 High priorities among children's rights (Papacostas 2009)	
Action	% indicating high priority
Providing more information to children about their rights and where to inquire about them (for instance, through information campaigns, or the creation of a website)	93.6
Giving more support to organizations working in the field of the protection of children's rights	92.4
Making a missing-children alert system operational throughout the European Union	87.7
Involving children more in the definition of policies that concern them – for instance, by organizing a Forum on these topics	78.4
Promoting children's rights in countries outside Europe	89.4

Another priority of the 15- to 18-year-old respondents is giving more support to organizations that seek to protect children's rights. Over 92% of the respondents indicated that giving more support to organizations working in the field of the protection of children's rights is a high priority. The survey does not inquire into kinds of support, but we can conjecture that the support would include financial support, cooperation with governing bodies, and access to facilities such as schools and detention facilities.

What are the best means to communicate young people's rights at the European level? These 15- to 18-year-old participants overwhelmingly responded that the Internet is the best means, at 70%. Correspondingly, over 20% recommended using TV programs, and a mere 7.6% recommended posting information in public libraries and school libraries. Studies of the Welsh Children's Commissioner and Iceland's Children's Ombudsman suggest that independent children's rights institutions can effectively advance information about children's rights. These organizations can request visits to schools, where they can discuss the work of ombudspersons and commissioners and remind young people what rights they possess. They can establish websites and other electronic means that use social media to disseminate information and news about young people's rights.

When young people think globally of children's rights

Inherently, children's rights are universal. As is true of human rights, a key feature of children's rights is that they belong to all children. Studies of young people's perspectives on their rights reveal that the majority of young people possess global understandings of the universality of their rights. Dr. Papacostas's Flash Eurobarometer studies indicate a high priority is to support promotion of young people's rights in non-European countries. Over 89% of the participants indicated this priority was high. Such an indication may suggest that young people living in the 27 EU member countries take a big-picture perspective when it comes to their situations and rights.

The researchers undertaking the comparisons of young people living in the Spanish Catalan region and the Italian Molise region asked participants whether they would support their teacher's decision to take time away from their classroom to teach in a "poor country." The gist of this question is whether young people are willing to forgo aspects of their own rights to benefit other young people – what the researchers call solidarity. Large proportions of young people in both countries (over 88% of Catalan participants and over 86% of Molise participants) expressed willingness to give up an aspect of their right to education in support of their teacher's decision and other young people's education.

That young people place high priority on others' rights is admirable. These findings suggest that young people often look beyond their own milieu, beyond the borders of their communities, to recognize and appreciate the global society in which they live. These high priorities may indicate that young people living in the European Union believe their governing systems are effective in implementing their rights. Perhaps the combination of their national governments, their local governments, the European Union government, and the UN is perceived as working better than other countries' combinatorial arrangements. Or perhaps this finding suggests misperceptions among European young people about how young people's rights work in other countries. This question is an empirical one that can be investigated. Many questions remain about young people's experiences with their rights and what meanings they ascribe to those rights.

Suppose participants in the Eurobarometer study are correct about their perceptions of needed changes in other countries. How can this priority be met? As you know, all UN member parties have ratified the UNCRC, with the exception of the United States. Therefore, UN treaty ratification is set. The challenge of promoting rights of young people living in other countries would mean other parts of the international framework of young people's rights require strengthening. It is plausible to assume that solving this dilemma does not require a one-size-fits-all approach. Instead, as we know, this challenge likely requires a young person's national government or local government to bolster its efforts, empowering NGOs to advocate effectively on behalf of young people, or a combination of these factors.

Other priorities when it comes to children's rights

Of course, other concerns and questions arise from children's rights discussions, even if they are not strictly inquiries about young people's rights. Dr. Papacostas, head of the Eurobarometer Unit, through the Flash Eurobarometer studies he directed, asked about areas in which young people's views should be considered when adopting legislation or making decisions. The participants in this study of 27 European countries identify education as a significant area, with a large proportion, 76%, of participants indicating education as a significant area. The next important area is security from violence, with over 42% indicating young people should be considered when adopting legislation or making decisions, followed by 41% indicating health and social affairs, such as public transport. The study participants seemed less concerned with some areas, such as justice (30%), sports and leisure (29%), the environment (21%), immigration (16.5%), and the media (12.4%). Participants in this Flash Eurobarometer study offered valuable insights into priorities involving young people's rights. Human rights experts stand to gain more information by conducting similar research across additional countries.

The next priority that Eurobarometer participants noted as important was making a missing-children alert system operational throughout the European Union. Over 87% of participants in this study placed high importance on this alert system. As of January 2020, a pan-European Union system is not in place. Still, steps are under way. A nonprofit organization, Amber Alert, has been established and is available in some European countries. The European Commission has established a telephone "hotline" individuals may call to report a missing child. In addition, the European Commission has established a child-alert mechanism that employs electronic communication, such as emails and telephone text messages, and motorway signs, to inform people of a missing child. As of January 2020, this child-alert mechanism was available in 17 European countries (European Commission 2020).

Sexual exploitation of young people is another problem these participants identify as a priority meriting attention. Nearly 20% of the participants in the 27 European countries identify sexual exploitation of young people as a significant problem. Like violence against children, sexual exploitation violates rights of bodily control and privacy. Occurrence of sexual exploitation and violence indicates governments' inabilities to protect young people when they are vulnerable to individuals who seek to do them harm. Among the participants, 13.6% place a high priority on tackling problems around racism and discrimination. A slightly lower proportion, 13.1%, point to poverty and social exclusion as a problem. A low proportion, nearly 4%, express concern about labor among young people.

The Eurobarometer participants were asked about tackling problems in their own countries. Nearly 23% of participants indicated their first priority is violence against children. This result is surprising, given existing legal and criminal justice systems in these European countries are believed to function comparatively well (World Justice Report 2019; Aromaa and Heiskanen 2008). This finding may bolster our concerns about Aristotle's state – that is, despite highly functioning legal and criminal justice systems, when it comes to domains where young people spend time, the state either struggles to enforce, or its officials are not interested in enforcing, young people's rights in the family home and other private domains. This concern, as we have discussed, has received significant attention from prominent scholars, including Martha Minow (2003).

Conclusion

Far from being irrelevant, children's rights mean something to young people. This chapter's overview of extant research on children's rights reveals that a singular, monolithic understanding of rights among young people does not exist. Research indicates that, even within a single country, young people can and do interpret rights differently.

Many young people believe rights are useful. While a surprisingly large number of young people are unaware of children's rights, across countries studied a large proportion recognize they possess rights and recognize what those rights are. Still, in these countries, many young people identify obstacles to exercising their rights.

A drawback to this chapter is that its analyses are confined, of course, to extant studies. We do enjoy the benefits and advantages from researchers having conducted multiple studies. The studies researchers have undertaken on children's rights are useful; some offer extraordinary insights into, and ideas about, children's rights. But we are limited. Studies have been primarily undertaken in Europe and Oceania. For many parts of the world, young people have not been invited to share thoughts about their experiences with rights, and what meanings they ascribe to those rights.

This need to expand social science research into other regions is an opportunity. Future research should attempt to conduct surveys, focus groups, and other approaches to gauge what young people think about their rights. We can pay attention to where young people live, the cultures in which they are growing up, and structures and social forces shaping their experiences with children's rights. We can anticipate discovering new evidence and new ideas when it comes to children's rights.

CHAPTER 5

What Do Children's Rights Do? What Children's Rights Are Missing?

Introduction

As we know, over a century, treaties, laws, organizations, and movements have pursued establishment and implementation of children's rights. While these significant undertakings are crucial, perhaps essential, to children's rights, we must ask what children's rights are able to accomplish (Reynaert, Bouverne-De Bie, and Vandevelde 2012). In this chapter, we will examine evidence of what children's rights can accomplish when it comes to their interests and well-being. Another task we will pursue is assessing whether advances in children's rights produce positive outcomes for adults (Alderson and John 2008). When young people's rights are widely available and implemented, do adults benefit? How? Through this chapter, we will investigate whether consequences of children's rights transcend national borders (Bentley 2005).

We will conclude this chapter with a discussion of what children's rights are "missing." The UNCRC and other important children's rights treaties may constrain debates of young people's rights, including the future of those rights. These treaties may effectively narrow perspectives of scholars, researchers, activists, government officials, and UN officials, even young people, when we deliberate on what rights belong to young people. How we think about young people and their interests will change, of course. New rights and rights we have overlooked will become part of global understandings of children's well-being. One example is the human right to science. Up until spring 2020, when the UN Committee on Economic, Social, and Cultural Rights (2020) published a General Comment on this topic, the human right to science had not received significant attention. Young people stand to benefit a great deal if their human right to science is enforced.

The right to have rights

Before analyzing what children's rights do, it is important to reflect on the importance of merely *possessing* rights. Recognition that one is the holder of rights is a marker of equal membership and standing. Entitlement to rights indicates that an individual is empowered to employ systems through which his or her rights can be exercised. Possessing rights means that one has the ability to exercise rights – the right to have rights.

In her book *The Alchemy of Race and Rights* (1992), Law professor Patricia Williams confronts arguments about the utility of law and rights that have been made by Critical Legal Studies (CLS). In sum, CLS scholars argue that the law benefits the powerful (Tushnet 1991). CLS scholars call for a shift from concentrating on rights to an examination of fundamental structures of society (Hutchinson and Monahan 1984). An implication we can draw is that CLS scholars contend that we should focus our energies on changing social–economic–political structures and relationships, rather than concentrating on rights as tools to produce social change for young people.

Williams responds to CLS scholars by asserting the importance of possessing rights. In contrast to exercising rights, which she does not oppose, Williams has in mind that possession of rights means an individual has access to the legal system writ large, and that that system recognizes this individual as holding the ability and power and resources to use the legal system. This person maintains legal standing. Possessing rights means the individual is a member of that society.

Williams shares the personal story that she and a colleague visited the faculty of a university located in a major US city. Her colleague was able to rent an apartment through a handshake with the landlord. He did not have to sign a lease, "put down" a deposit of funds, or demonstrate that his bank account held enough funds for rent. Instead, the landlord gave the colleague a key to the apartment, and that was it. Factors that establish a legal relationship, such as executing a contract, were omitted from this exchange. The colleague and the landlord did not take steps necessary to employing rights in court. In contrast, before Williams was able to rent an apartment, the landlord did a credit check, wanted records of her bank account, required a deposit, and required that Williams sign a lease. These steps represented establishment of a legal relationship between Williams and the landlord. If for some reason the relationship faltered, Williams and the landlord were prepared to exercise their rights and enjoy legal standing in court.

Williams explained to her colleague that she was glad to take these steps. To Williams, these steps represented the landlord's recognition of her legal abilities to sign a lease, a contract. In turn, Williams said that signing a contract meant that the landlord recognized Williams could employ the legal system if the landlord and she experienced differences over the contract and its fulfillment. This ability to participate and deploy the legal system and the landlord's recognition of that fact meant that Williams could take these steps, indicating she is a member of that society. She held standing the same as anyone else in the society. As a Black American woman, Williams appreciated not only the ability to participate and deploy these rights, but also the landlord's recognition of these abilities, for they indicate that she has overcome legal barriers that are designed to limit individuals' abilities to fully participate and exercise their rights. These steps represented possession of rights and abilities to exercise those rights, if needed, through the legal system. Williams's experience indicates she enjoys equal membership and standing.

This membership is the same membership that received T. H. Marshall's attention (Marshall 1950). Membership is a key feature of Marshall's ideas of citizenship rights. Marshall reasoned that fulfillment of citizenship rights would lead to an individual's membership in that society's civilization. Through possessing this bundle of citizenship rights, an individual is empowered to participate in society and enjoy the same benefits as every other member of that civilization.

Repudiation of the right to possess rights can lead to denial of equal membership and standing. This dilemma was the focus of Hannah Arendt's work, including a 1949 *New Yorker* article and her 1951 book, *The Origins of Totalitarianism*. Through her study of Nazi leaders of a nation state taking steps to remove the right to have rights from a social group, such as Jewish people, Arendt argues that, by removing a right to have rights, the Nazis reduced the ability to challenge their leadership. When those rights were eliminated, the Nazis were able to run the German nation state without having to pay attention to or complying with rules attached to rights. Individuals could not assert rights to exert control over the Nazi nation state.

In her book, *The Rights of Others*, Benhabib employs Arendt's ideas to consider the predicament of individuals who are not living in their native nation states. Immigrants and refugees often cannot exercise citizenship rights due to their statuses. Rather than a nation state without rules, such as the German state the Nazis tried to build, immigrants and refugees must contend with a receiving nation state that does not necessarily recognize rules and procedures that apply to them. It is for this reason that Benhabib argues for extending a right to have rights to members of these groups. Ultimately, unless immigrants and refugees possess a right to have rights, they cannot fully enjoy the civilization of the society that has received them. They possess neither membership nor standing, and have been received, but not accepted as members of the society.

These ideas apply to young people. The UDHR, as well as human rights treaties, indicate that young people possess the same rights as every other person. The UNCRC, a separate human rights treaty articulating rights belonging to young people, re-states civil, political, social, economic, and participation rights. These treaties indicate that young people are members of their societies in the same way as other citizens. These treaties indicate that young people possess the right to have rights.

Or do they? In this chapter, we examine impacts of rights on young people. We take a closer look at whether young people enjoy outcomes that we expect rights to produce. We then return to these ideas to consider whether young people are full members of their societies, or whether their predicament in society is that rights-based rules do not apply in the nation states in which they live. Does a right to have rights mean much to young people?

Now we will review major organizations and aspects of the international framework of children's rights to consider their impacts on these rights. At base, we ask whether these components matter to children's rights.

UN Committee

Organizations with rules, procedures, and norms have been established to foster the membership and standing of young people, at least regarding their rights. Here we will examine these organizations and their accompanying institutional frameworks to assess whether they are successful at fostering membership and standing of young people and their rights.

A key approach to ensuring that young people's rights are implemented and that young people enjoy membership and standing is through the efforts of UN organizations. Chief among organizations that monitor young people's rights is the UN Committee on the Rights of the Child (UN Committee). As we know, the UN Committee consists of 18 independent experts. These experts are responsible for monitoring efforts of national governments that have ratified the UN Convention.

How does the UN Committee effectuate children's rights? The primary means are engaging States parties and monitoring their efforts to implement young people's rights. Are these means effective? Let's review the process.

As we discussed earlier, the UNCRC requires that a national government file its report with the UN Committee within two years of ratification, and again every five years after (UNCRC Article 44, paragraph 1). This process is key to ascertaining whether national governments take young people's rights seriously. Adhering to this procedure is key to determining whether young people possess membership and standing. If the process is a failure, we may conclude that young people do not enjoy membership and standing, and their rights are not being implemented. We may also conclude that the process is not working, and perhaps a different approach is needed if we do desire membership, standing, and rights implementation for young people.

As of 2004, 15 years after the UNCRC entered into force, the UN Committee reported that 180 States parties had filed their initial reports, 85 had filed their second reports, and 11 had filed their third reports; 192 States had ratified or acceded to the UNCRC. By 2019, 30 years following adoption, all states should have filed their two-year reports, and all but 2, Somalia and South Sudan, are expected to have submitted at least one five-year report. Instead, we find numerous States parties that have failed to file reports in a timely manner. For example, Afghanistan filed its first report, due in 1996, in 2009. Similarly, Lesotho filed its first report 4 years late, then its second report 17 years late. On the other hand, Denmark has filed each report in the year it was due. The aforementioned failures to file reports suggest that States parties do not take seriously their commitment to young people's rights. These failures are indictments of this international framework of young people's rights, suggesting that the UN system fails to support fully young people's membership and standing.

The Committee typically invites nine States parties to present their reports at each session. When organizing these sessions, the Committee organizes presentations according to chronological order of report submissions, giving priority to States parties that have filed their initial reports. That means that the States parties who are most delinquent in filing go first in making their reports.

For each State party's report, the Committee allocates one day to public examination of the report. That one day consists of two meetings that are each 3 hours in length. The Committee then spends 2 to 3 hours meeting privately to prepare its Concluding Observations for the State party

(Working Methods, United Nations Committee on the Rights of the Child 2020).

As the Committee reviews a State party's report before the session, it holds a "pre-session working group" in which a working group of the Committee leads a meeting with representatives of UN agencies and bodies, NGOs, national human rights institutions, and young people's organizations. At this stage, these groups have submitted information to the Committee about the particular State party and its report. The pre-session working group produces a "List of Issues" that is expected to give the government insights into what Committee members will discuss with government representatives.

The State party's report is then discussed before the Committee at the public meeting. Serving as rapporteurs, two UN Committee members have the responsibility of determining the situation of young people's rights in the particular country. Representatives of other UN agencies are permitted to participate. Any individual can attend, but he or she cannot participate. NGO representatives may attend, as well as members of the media.

A representative of the State party makes an introductory statement, then the Committee's chair asks the rapporteur or rapporteurs to review the state of children's rights in the country of the State party. Committee members may ask questions or offer comments to which the representatives of the State party can respond. Prior to the end of the meeting, the rapporteurs offer a summary of their observations and discussions held during the meeting, as well as their recommendations. Representatives of the State party are then invited to make a final statement.

After the meeting, the Committee prepares its Concluding Observations. These meetings are not open. The Concluding Observations usually include discussions of progress the State party has achieved, but typically concentrate on problems, including obstacles, and factors that have slowed implementation. When the Concluding Observations are filed, they are shared with the State party and become official documents. States parties are supposed to make the Concluding Observations available to their residents, thereby making the national government accountable to the public in improving protections and monitoring of children's rights.

Typically, young people do not have the opportunity to participate in these meetings. They are not entitled to receive the Concluding Observations any more than anyone else. The UN Committee does not convey the Concluding Observations in language and formats accessible to young people of all ages. We can conclude that the UN Committee considers the audience of its Concluding Observations not to be the young people on whose behalf they serve, but national governments and civil society actors that are expected to serve as watchdogs of young people's rights.

Concluding Observations and young people's rights

Given that the audience of the Concluding Observations is outside the halls of the United Nations, do Concluding Observations matter to young people's rights? Here we will examine whether national governments respond to Concluding Observations.

Overall, the British government seems to consider the Concluding Observations. In June 2016, the UN Committee published its Concluding Observations on the UK report. In October 2016, Edward Timpson, the Minister of State for Vulnerable Children and Families, encouraged Members of the House of Commons to take seriously the Concluding Observations by reflecting the voice of the child fully in the design and implementation of policy. Minister Timpson (2016) asserted the following:

> Both the UNCRC articles and Concluding Recommendations serve as a helpful and important guide to making sure that our policies – whether they hold direct or indirect consequences – consider children. My Department will issue the Committee's Concluding Recommendations across Whitehall this week. I encourage all Departments to read these recommendations and take them into account as we work together to achieve social mobility.

Despite this British leader's attention to the Concluding Observations, at best the evidence is mixed that the British government is heeding the UN Committee. Appearing to ignore the Concluding Observations, the British government took steps to establish a new welfare system that harmed young people (Kingsley 2018a, 2018b). In spite of the UN Committee's call, the British government is making budget cuts through austerity program that directly harms young people.

In its Concluding Observations to Norway, the UN Committee noted that Norway's municipal approach to delivering services to young people was hampered by funding mechanisms and that young people do not possess rights to welfare services. In response, the Norwegian government changed this approach. Young people are now entitled to welfare services through the Children's Welfare Act (Søvig 2019). The Norwegian government seems to have taken seriously the Concluding Observations of the UN Committee.

Because of censorship, individuals living in some countries will not be aware of the UN Committee's Concluding Observations of their national governments' efforts to implement the UNCRC. For example, in preparation for the Chinese government appearing before the Committee, in November 2012, Tibet Watch and Free Tibet filed a joint report to the Committee about its concerns with children's rights in China. In their Concluding Observations, the UN Committee noted its deep concern with the "continuous violations of the rights of and discrimination against Tibetan and Uighur children" (Tibet Watch 2020). The Committee noted these young people were experiencing violations of their freedoms of religion, language, and culture. The Committee also flagged violations regarding detention and torture.

Unfortunately, the Chinese government's response through their Final Comments on the Concluding Observations was to reject these concerns (Comments of the Chinese Government about the Concluding Observations on the Combined 3rd & 4th Periodic Reports of China, Adopted by the CRC Committee at its 64th Session). Instead, the Chinese government indicated the Committee's concerns were exaggerated and not based on facts. Given the reputation that NGOs in China are weak and government control of the press is strong, it is unlikely that the Chinese government will respond to these concerns. Tibet Watch notes China was to file its next report in March 2019. The Chinese government failed to file this report.

One way the Concluding Observations matter to young people's rights is in relation to NGOs trying to hold national governments accountable through publicizing the Concluding Observations. For example, one effort of the Children's Rights Alliance for England is to hold the national government accountable to the UN Committee's Concluding Observations. Since 2003, the Alliance has annually published its State of Children's Rights in England, which the Alliance treats as an important way to hold the UK government accountable to the Convention and to the Committee's Concluding Observations. The Alliance's 2018 report emphasized that the resources devoted to Brexit and the government's attention to Brexit were taking away its attention from children's rights (Children's Rights Alliance for England 2018).

On June 23, 2013, the Legal Center for Arab Minority Rights in Israel published the Committee's Concluding Observations on Israel's implementation of the CRC. In particular, the Center challenged the Israeli government to follow through on the Concluding Observations on Israel's violations of the health and education rights of Palestinian Arab Bedouin children (Adalah 2013). The Center had raised this point and others by filing an NGO report to the UN Committee, as well as through submitting a response to the Israeli government's reply to the Committee's List of Issues. As a watchdog and advocate, the Legal Center for Arab Minority Rights is attempting to ensure that the Israeli government follows through on the UN Committee's Concluding Observations.

The evidence of governments acting on Concluding Observations is mixed. As we saw with the national government of China's rejection of the Concluding Observations, some governments dismiss the UN Committee's recommendations, while others, such as the Norwegian government, seem to embrace Concluding Observations. Even so, we have reason to believe that there are other governments whose responses are motivated by pressures from NGOs.

Because young people do not have a direct role in assembling reports of States parties or in the UN Committee's process, and do not necessarily receive the Concluding Observations, their membership and standing are advanced only indirectly and secondarily.

Other UN bodies

Of course, the UN is made up of additional committees that are responsible for implementing other UN treaties. Do young people experience membership and standing and advancement of their rights through efforts of these other UN committees? Does the UN Committee on the Rights of the Child work with other UN committees?

The UN Committee on the Rights of the Child has collaborated with other UN committees to publish General Comments. These General Comments reflect mutual objectives and responsibilities of the committees. So far, these General Comments have been jointly prepared by the UN Committee on the Rights of the Child and one other committee. That is, the General Comments are the work of two UN committees, not three or more.

As we have discussed, the UN Committee on the Rights of the Child has collaborated with the UN Committee on the Protection of the Rights of All Migrant Workers and Members of Their Families (CMW), and the UN Committee on Eliminating Discrimination against Women (CEDAW). With the CMW, the UN Committee on the Rights of the Child has published one General Comment (no. 3 of the CMW and no. 22 of the UNCRC) on "General Principles" and another General Comment (no. 4 of the CMW and no. 23 of the UNCRC) on transit and destination. With the CEDAW, the UN Committee on the Rights of the Child has published one General Comment (no. 31 of the CEDAW and no. 18 of the UNCRC) on harmful practices.

The rights of young people, namely their membership and standing, are complicated when a young person is involved in international migration. Joint General Comment CMW No. 3 – CRC No. 22 (2017) concentrates on principles when it comes to protecting rights of young people who are connected to international migration. This Joint General Comment rejects collective expulsion and re-foulement: group expulsion to the country where the migrant may face persecution. It notes that young people may face multiple vulnerabilities when it comes to international migration. That is, a young person may be a migrant; may be born to a migrant parent in a destination country, thereby not being "from" their parent's native country; or a young person may stay in their origin country while a parent migrates to another country (paragraph 3). In each situation, a young person may experience vulnerabilities not only because of predicaments and vulnerabilities due to their own statuses, but also because of the vulnerabilities of the people on whom they rely and on whom their legal standing may rest. This situation highlights reasons for concern about the right to have rights, articulated by Arendt and Benhabib in their aforementioned works. It is this right to have rights that demonstrates the importance and need of human rights that transcend borders of jurisdictions that will not take citizenship rights seriously, including young people's citizenship rights.

The CMW and the UN Committee have jointly published CMW General Comment No. 4 (2017) and UNCRC General Comment No. 23 (2017). This Joint General Comment states that governments should assess each young person as an individual, and should keep in mind that young person's best interests. That means that a decision to return a young person to his or her origin country should be made on a case-by-case basis (paragraph 33). The Joint General Comment calls on national governments to prohibit and abolish detention of child and family migrants. The Joint General Comment also calls on national governments to restrict use of personal data belonging to young people (paragraph 17). This UN document reminds parties that non-discrimination is a basis of migration practices that affect young people and their rights (paragraph 22). Arbitrary interference into a family's life and its privacy can arise from detention and deportation. However, the General Comment does not

specify roles of young people and concern for their participation in these efforts, which undermines their membership
and standing.

The UN Committee on the Rights of the Child has
published a General Comment with the UN Committee
on the Elimination of Discrimination against Women
(CEDAW). While all but one UN member has ratified the
UN Convention on the Rights of the Child – the United
States – CEDAW also enjoys wide ratification, with only
six UN members not having ratified CEDAW, including
Iran, Palau, Somalia, Sudan, Tonga, and the United States.
This General Comment, the thirty-first comment published
by CEDAW and the eighteenth of the UNCRC, focuses on
harmful practices. The harmful practices receiving attention
from the UNCRC and CEDAW are tied to violence against
women and children, such as female genital mutilation,
child and forced marriage, extreme dietary restrictions,
and medical treatment and plastic surgery (paragraphs 6
and 9). Together, the committees contend that "effective
prevention and elimination of harmful practices require
... well-defined, rights-based and locally relevant holistic
strategy that includes supportive legal and policy measures,
including social measures that are combined with commen-
surate political commitment and accountability at all levels"
(paragraph 33). Further, the committees call for horizontal
and vertical strategies (paragraph 34). This approach seems
to mean expecting "all relevant public stakeholders" – both
public and private actors and organizations at local, regional,
and national levels – to be responsible for preventing these
harmful practices. However, this Joint General Comment
does not specify the roles of young people and concern for
their participation in these efforts, which undermines their
membership and standing.

As an example, the committees point to the "clear corre-lation" between "low educational attainment of girls and women and the prevalence of harmful practices" (paragraph 62). The committees call on States parties to provide universal, free, compulsory primary school education. Particularly, the committees express concern about women who "drop out," and those who live in remote communities, when it comes to this education (paragraph 62). The joint efforts of these different UN committees may prove crucial to bringing attention to violations of human and children's rights. Their collaborative efforts may prevent violations of rights beyond the conventions they are charged with monitoring.

UN agencies

The UN is a vast organization consisting of multiple agencies. Do these organizations work on behalf of young people's rights? Do young people hold membership and standing within these agencies? Here we review major UN agencies whose work influences the lives and well-being of children across the world.

Established in 1946, UNICEF, the United Nations Children's Fund (formerly the United Nations International Children's Emergency Fund), is *the* UN agency tasked with advancing rights of young people. Working all over the world, UNICEF works on child protection and inclusion, child survival, and education. It seeks to eliminate gender discrimination, respond to emergencies, and promote innovation (United Nations Children's Fund n.d.c). One aspect of UNICEF that is central to children's rights is the research and analysis UNICEF under-takes. Each year, UNICEF publishes its State of the World's Children report. A challenge facing UNICEF's research team is that they do not enjoy autonomy to focus on research that their work indicates is crucial. Instead, other UN agencies can request that the research team undertake a research project of importance to that UN agency. This problem undermines the efforts of the UNICEF research team. It is clear that this team deserves greater support and autonomy so that comprehensive, reliable, and valid understandings of young people and their rights are available globally.

UNICEF is a custodian of 7, and co-custodian of 10, Sustainable Development Goals (SDGs). The SDGs are 17 goals that will eliminate or reduce global social problems, ranging from eliminating poverty to equality to sustainable energy to water (United Nations 2020) (see figure 5.1). As custodian and co-custodian, UNICEF supports political leadership of all countries in "generating, analyzing and using data for" SDG indicators (United Nations Children's Fund n.d.b).

The United Nations Educational, Scientific and Cultural Organization (UNESCO) supports young people's rights in many ways. Its efforts to advance education, promote science, and other efforts have supported young people's rights. UNESCO's Youth Programme is organized to include young people between the ages of 15 and 24 in various UNESCO activities. One activity of the Youth Programme is working with national governments to include young people in development of national policies surrounding education, science, culture, and communication (UNESCO n.d.). In addition, UNESCO has sponsored various programs that concentrate its support on young people's rights. In November 2016, UNESCO held a CAMPUS program that examined exclusion of young people from rights. CAMPUS programs are conferences where young people can debate specific issues. UNESCO has also shone a spotlight on the work of Kailash Satyarthi, who has advocated for young people's freedom from economic exploitation, forced labor, and human trafficking (de Sousa 2018). UNESCO does not seem to involve participation of people younger than age 15 in its activities. This failure means UNESCO does not directly engage approximately 25% of the world's population, a loss to these young people, their futures, and the societies in which they will grow up and become adults.

The Food and Agriculture Organization of the United Nations (FAO) focuses on collecting, analyzing, and disseminating information about food, nutrition, and agriculture. As such, the FAO does consider the importance of young people's rights when it comes to these objectives. The FAO has publicly called for protections of young people's rights when it comes to labor practices. It seems that the FAO concentrates on

Figure 5.1   Young people's freedom from economic exploitation continues to be violated. This photo shows young boys working at a mine in the Democratic Republic of the Congo. (Photo: Julien Harneis / Wikimedia Commons)

three aspects of child labor, including publicizing that young people are not to perform agricultural work (with exceptions), promoting approaches to monitoring agricultural labor among young people (which the FAO acknowledges is difficult to monitor), and providing support so that reasons for relying on young people to perform agricultural work are alleviated (FAO n.d.). In cooperation with Save the Children, the FAO has also published on property rights of young people, including rights of inheritance (Save the Children and FAO 2009). This work focuses on "property grabbing" in some sub-Saharan countries. Property grabbing is the practice of seizing the property of a deceased person and preventing that property from transferring to the person or people to whom the property now belongs.

As its name suggests, the International Labour Organization of the United Nations (ILO) focuses on labor practices (International Labour Organization 2004). The ILO has given attention to rights of young people in relation to work (International Labour Organization 2017b). The ILO has strived to ensure that young people are protected from inappropriate labor practices, including freedom from hazardous work (International Labour Organization 2003, 2017a). The International Monetary Fund (IMF) works with individual countries to ensure their governments' budgets lead to overall growth and employment improvements. The IMF has worked with governments so that their budgets take into account expenses associated with young people's rights, such as establishing universal primary education for all young people (IMF 2018a, 2018b). The IMF also works to promote education of young people, which it views as a strategy of long-term poverty reduction (Hillman and Jenkner 2004). The World Bank strives to foster the economic capacity of individual countries through providing loans, credit, and grants. Similar to the IMF, the World Bank has advocated for young people's rights to education (Betcherman, Fares, Luinstra, and Prouty 2004). In addition, the World Bank has called for national identification of every child (World Bank n.d.). The World Bank posits that, without this identification, many young people are denied services to which they have rights. Even as these three organizations are recognized for their efforts to promote safe labor practices, employment stability, and economic security, all have embraced children's rights as part of their work.

The World Health Organization (WHO) advocates for children's rights to health and development (World Health Organization 2014). It comes as no surprise that the WHO's understanding of children's rights to health is broadly conceived. The WHO strives to reduce child mortality, tackle disease, fight malnutrition, prevent violence, support young people with disabilities, and works to end female genital mutilation and forced marriage. The WHO's efforts to produce superior health outcomes incorporate children's rights. The International Committee of the Red Cross calls for protections and implementation of rights of young people who are living in humanitarian crises. These efforts of the Red Cross harken back to the work and objectives of the sisters whose work resulted in the first Geneva Convention.

This review demonstrates that many UN agencies recognize that rights of young people are useful – perhaps necessary – to achieving agency goals. The work of these UN agencies is far reaching, both in terms of people they serve and how they serve those people. Framing and employing children's rights as key to the work these agencies achieve may produce lasting impacts for young people and full membership in their societies.

UN Special Procedures

The Special Procedures of the Human Rights Council are independent human rights experts possessing mandates to report and advise on human rights. Appointed by the Human Rights Council, Special Procedures are either an individual, called a "Special Rapporteur," or a working group. These individuals serve in individual capacities, meaning they are not UN staff members and are not financially compensated. They are expected to maintain independence, impartiality, and integrity as they competently and efficiently fulfill their mandated functions. Each individual is limited to holding the office for six years.

The work of some of the independent human rights experts is described below. Country-specific experts focus on a dozen countries: Belarus, Cambodia, Central African Republic, Eritrea, Iran, North Korea, Mali, Myanmar, Palestine, Somalia, Sudan, and Syria. These experts undertake their work through country visits, communications, and other activities. Country visits only take place at the invitation of States. If an invitation is received, the expert can undertake a country visit. Governments of some countries have extended "standing invitations" to experts. A standing invitation means the government is prepared to receive a visit. Experts will participate with government officials about findings from their visit. Based on the visit, the expert will file a report to the Human Rights Council.

Often, experts receive allegations of human rights violations. They are permitted to communicate with national governments, as well as non-state actors, about these allegations. They are allowed to seek information, provide observations, and make recommendations.

These experts do pursue other activities. They may prepare standards and guidelines surrounding human rights, participate in consultations, as well as seminars and conferences, and undertake other types of visits, including ones that provide technical assistance and raise public awareness.

The mandate of some Special Rapporteurs incorporates a focus on young people's rights. The Special Rapporteur on the sale and sexual exploitation of children, including child prostitution, child pornography and other child sexual abuse material, publishes media advisories and press releases, and conducts missions. These missions are to individual countries, during which the Special Rapporteur assesses the work of the particular national government in preventing the sale and sexual exploitation of young people. These assessments include recommendations as to how the government may allocate resources, amend procedures, and work with civil-society actors to improve circumstances of young people experiencing sexual exploitation, as seen in the 2018 report of the Special Rapporteur on sustainable environments, "Report on the Rights of Children and the Environment." The Special Rapporteur on safe drinking water and sanitation has organized Youth Challenges, which are online programs that raise awareness of rights to safe drinking water and sanitation. The Special Rapporteur on environmentally sound management has reported on children's rights and hazardous substances and wastes. The Rapporteur has identified how children's rights are violated when state and non-state entities expose young people to toxic chemicals.

Although these Special Procedures, including Special Rapporteurs, often focus on specific kinds of human rights concerns, such as access to safe drinking water, many consider rights of young people in their work. These Special Procedures can bring valuable perspectives and insights on children's rights that other bodies, including the UN Committee, may not be able to provide.

Patterns of young people's rights

This chapter has presented evidence of structures, organizations, rules, and processes that are indicative of what children's rights may achieve. To ascertain the status of children's rights, a starting point may be to see whether a national government has incorporated the UNCRC into national law. Table 5.1 presents evidence that the Children's Rights Information Network (CRIN) published in 2016 on whether a national government has incorporated the Convention into national law (Children's Rights Information Network 2016).[1]

There are 94 countries that have incorporated the CRC into national law. In contrast, as the table shows, 73 countries have not incorporated the CRC into national law, and 28 have partially incorporated the CRC into national law. That is, almost half of the countries that have ratified the Convention have incorporated the Convention into national law. This indicator appears to provide evidence that, in many countries, young people possess the right to have rights, enjoying membership and standing. However, if we reflect on the expectations of the Convention, we recall that CRC ratification requires that a national government incorporate the CRC into national law. In many countries, therefore, young people do not possess the right to have rights articulated in the Convention.

As you know, the right to education is articulated in Article 28 of the Convention. The right to education permits a young person to go through the process of receiving an education. Despite this clear articulation, evidence suggests great differences in resources devoted to education across countries. Table 5.2 presents information about government expenditures on

[1] The author thanks Leo Ratledge of CRIN for sharing CRIN information about Convention incorporation.

Table 5.1 National governments which have not, or only partially, incorporated the UNCRC into national law (CRIN 2016)

Partially incorporated	Not incorporated	
Algeria	Afghanistan	Malta
Belarus	Antigua and Barbuda	Marshall Islands
Belgium	Australia	Mauritius
Belize	Austria	Micronesia
Croatia	Bahamas	Myanmar/Burma
Czech Republic	Bangladesh	Nauru
France	Barbados	New Zealand
Guyana	Botswana	Nigeria
Iran	Brunei Darussalam	Pakistan
Japan	Cambodia	Palau
Jordan	Canada	Palestine
Kuwait	Central African Republic	Papua New Guinea
Liechtenstein	China	Philippines
Luxembourg	Comoros	Saint Kitts and Nevis
Mali	Côte d'Ivoire	Saint Lucia
Mauritania	Cuba	Saint Vincent and the Grenadines
Monaco	Denmark	Samoa
Morocco	Dominica	Seychelles
Netherlands	Eritrea	Singapore
Oman	Fiji	Solomon Islands
Poland	Gambia	Somalia
Qatar	Ghana	South Africa
Saudi Arabia	Grenada	South Sudan
South Korea	Guinea-Bissau	Sri Lanka
Switzerland	India	Swaziland
Syria	Indonesia	Sweden
Turkey	Iraq	Tanzania
Uganda	Ireland	Thailand
	Israel	Tonga
	Jamaica	Trinidad & Tobago
	Kiribati	Tuvalu
	Laos	United Arab Emirates
	Lesotho	United Kingdom
	Liberia	United States
	Malawi	Zambia
	Malaysia	Zimbabwe
	Maldives	

Table 5.2 Number of countries with government expenditure per student, primary education, by % of GDP per capita (World Bank 2020)

Percent	Number of countries
0–4.9	7
5–9.9	41
10–14.9	50
15–19.9	38
20–24.9	32
25–29.9	2
30–34.9	5
35–39.9	1
40–44.9	1
45–49.9	1

primary education per capita (World Bank 2020 – for a full table with data listed by country, see the appendix). While information is not available for some countries, the percentage of per capita expenditures ranges from below 5% (Kazakhstan 0.2%; Monaco 3.3%; Central African Republic 4.1%; Rwanda 4.3%; South Sudan 4.6%; Guinea-Bissau and Gabon 4.7%) to greater than 35% (Djibouti 37.3%; Serbia 43.7%; Cuba 49.1%).

Discrimination can occur when young people exercise their rights to education. Two individuals may have different experiences in exercising these rights. Why does that matter? Discrimination matters for multiple reasons. One reason is because human rights are non-discriminatory, a "foundation of international human rights law" (www.ohchr.org/EN/Issues/Discrimination/Pages/discrimination.aspx). Second, discrimination means that one person is enjoying a right while another person is not. UNICEF has determined that, in some countries, boys and girls have different ages to which they must remain enrolled in school. This difference means one group is receiving less education than the other group. This difference in formal schooling may lead to differences in secondary and tertiary educational opportunities, employment opportunities, and literacy and math abilities.

As noted in Article 24, the right to health should lead to superior health outcomes. For instance, in countries whose national governments have ratified the Convention, it is reasonable to anticipate the positive result of superior health outcomes when the right to health is implemented. The reported proportion of children who are born with low weights (LBW; table 5.3 – for a full table with data listed by country, see the appendix) ranges from a high of 35% for the country of Mauritania to lows of 4% and below for Albania, China, Finland, Iceland, and South Korea. LBW does not result from a child failing to take care of herself. Instead, scientists have determined that parents' health leads to LBW. This outcome reminds us that young people's rights are interconnected to others' rights. In the case of LBW, this is the right to health possessed and exercised by the child's parents.

Table 5.3 Number of countries with low-birthweight babies by % of births (World Bank 2020)

Percent	Number of countries
0–4.9	6
5–9.9	86
10–14.9	68
15–19.9	16
20–24.9	7
25–29.9	5
30–34.9	3
35+	1

The right to nationality, articulated in the Convention's Article 7, paragraph 1, states: "The child shall be registered immediately after birth and shall have the right from birth to a name, the right to acquire a nationality and. as far as possible, the right to know and be cared for by his or her parents." The right to nationality provides membership and standing to a young person. In this case, Arendt would predict that a person may experience difficulties exercising other rights if he or she does not possess this right to nationality. It is important to note that the right to obtain nationality varies across countries. In some countries, the right to nationality varies by social group membership. One group membership that often matters is whether the individual is a child.

Age limitations shape many rights – most prominent is the right to vote and participate in the country's electoral system. As we have discussed, while the right to vote is considered a key political right, most young people are ineligible to vote across the world. The same is true of the right to become a candidate for political office, as well as to hold an office.

Freedom from economic exploitation is an economic right that protects young people. Many governments have outlawed employment of young people except in particular circumstances, such as part-time employment that does not interfere with exercising the right to education. Indeed, many authorities consider the right to education to bolster freedom from economic exploitation. If a young person is enrolled in school, then he or she should be able to avoid economic exploitation. A person can only be in one place at a time.

UNICEF estimates indicate great differences across the world in the proportion of people aged 5 to 17 who are working. In Benin, 54% of young men are working, and we find the same proportion of young women working in Somalia. UNICEF established averages by region. The highest average is 32% for young men and young women in West and Central Africa. Across all regions, UNICEF reports that young men are less likely to experience freedom from economic exploitation than young women. However, young women, more than young men, do not experience freedom from economic exploitation in some countries. These include Angola, Belarus, Burundi, CAR, Chad, Comoros, Costa Rica, Côte d'Ivoire, Democratic Republic of the Congo, Guinea-Bissau, Laos, Macedonia, Mozambique, Nepal, Nigeria, Rwanda, Sao Tome and Principe, Somalia, Tajikistan, Vanuatu, and Yemen. This evidence suggests that, in many places, young people do not enjoy freedom from economic exploitation, a critical right for their current and future well-being.

Young people possess rights to be free from harm. For example, Article 19 of the UNCRC states that a young person enjoys protections from violence, injury, abuse, neglect, maltreatment, and exploitation when that young person is in the care of a parent, legal guardian, or another person who takes care of the young person. Correspondingly, opponents of female genital mutilation (FGM) have used Article 19 to call on national governments to ban this practice. UNICEF reports that, while FGM still takes place in some countries, a noticeable decline has occurred in the last 10 years. Arguably, this decline is due to articulation and advocacy of young people's freedoms from harm.

UNICEF (2016) reports that young women up to age 14 experienced female genital mutilation or cutting, FGM/C, across a range of countries for the five-year period 2010 to 2015. In Gambia, 56% of young women (data are to age 14) experienced FGM. Table 5.4 presents UNICEF (2016) estimates.

All 21 countries represented in this table are States parties to the UNCRC. Not one country has filed reservations to the

Table 5.4 Proportion of girls up to age 14 who have experienced FGM/C (United Nations Children's Fund 2016)

Country	Percent
Gambia	56
Mauritania	54
Indonesia	49
Guinea	46
Eritrea	33
Sudan	32
Guinea-Bissau	30
Ethiopia	24
Nigeria	17
Yemen	15
Egypt	14
Burkina Faso	13
Sierra Leone	13
Senegal	13
Côte d'Ivoire	10
Kenya	3
Uganda	1
Central African Republic	1
Ghana	1
Togo	0.3
Benin	0.2

UNCRC indicating distinct perspectives on FGM from their commitments to young people's rights. The continued practice of FGM is made all the more troubling when one considers the notion that FGM is practiced on young women, and that the UNCRC places responsibilities on young people's parents, guardians, and caretakers to ensure their well-being.

Similarly, male circumcision is defined as "surgical removal of the skin covering the tip of the penis" (Mayo Clinic 2018). Although male circumcision has not received the same attention from human rights advocates, some experts contend that male circumcision is a human rights violation. Svoboda (2013) argues that male circumcision violates a person's right to bodily integrity. He identifies provisions in the UDHR, the UNCRC, the ICCPR, and the Convention against Torture that prohibit male circumcision. As has been seen in UNICEF's work on FGM, Svoboda predicts that once male circumcision rates fall below a specific level, acceptance of male circumcision will also drop. At what level that will occur, however, is not clear.

A 2010 World Health Organization report identifies great variation in reported male circumcision across the world for 2006. This report identifies prevalence of male circumcision to be between 20 and 80% in Australia, the United States, and other countries, but prevalence is higher than 80% in many African countries, including Mauritius. On the other hand, this report identifies prevalence to be 20% or less in many western European countries and Asian countries. If male circumcision is to be treated as a violation of children's rights similar to FGM, cultural practices must be changed in many societies.

Experts have examined the right to participation from multiple perspectives. Ultimately, what experts want to know is whether young people have the right to participate in organizations and activities affecting their well-being. To consider this perspective, we must examine whether young people have rights to participate in systems where their civil, political, and social rights are exercised. For example, the right to bodily control is often considered a civil right. Many national governments have banned corporal punishment of young people. While the ban is part of the process of preventing physical punishment of young people, little evidence is available on whether the ban works in practice.

Many offices of children's ombudspersons and commissioners have set up advisory groups whose members are young people. The Iceland Children's Ombudsman accepts applications from any young person living in Iceland between the ages of 13 and 17. The advisory group meets monthly. Other independent children's rights institutions have taken similar approaches.

What do young people's rights do for adults?

While the focus of young people's rights is young people, do young people's rights benefit adults? Do some particular rights articulated for young people advance rights of adults? The right to a formal education has many implications for the lives of adults. This right shifts responsibilities for providing a formal education to the government. Beyond removing financial responsibility from parents' shoulders, abundant evidence indicates that formal education leads to economic improvements, reductions in inequality, and stronger communities committed to human rights.

An important instance of when young people's rights may benefit adults and their rights is regarding freedom from corporal punishment. Academics and researchers have presented strong evidence that young people experiencing violence may have higher odds of acting violently against others, including young people, when reaching adulthood (Straus, Gelles, and Steinmetz 2006). The opportunity to grow up without experiencing physical violence may help to reduce violence not only later in the victim's life, but in others' lives.

Competence is key to various aspects of children's lives, from making medical decisions to making legal decisions and being fairly treated in criminal justice systems (Mutcherson 2006). For some time, judges and other authorities defined competence according to age (Willard 1982). That is, a decision maker made conclusions about competence to make medical and legal decisions on the basis of chronological age. Across many countries, determinations of competence now are made in consideration of an individual's qualities and personality. Rather than make a decision on competence according to a child's age, authorities now try to assess the child, her capabilities, and her desires. This holistic approach to competence of a child has been extended to determinations of the competence of adults.

A child's best interests are considered a paramount concern in assessing what should be done for young people. Increasingly, courts are going beyond laws and judicial holdings to consider more broadly what a child's best interests are (Long and Sephton 2011; Welch and Jones 2018). In addition to turning to input from family members, counselors, social workers, and others, judges and other decision makers are asking young people what they think is best (Watts 2004). These approaches are increasingly being used in other forums. Judges and court officials are seeking input from social workers and other professionals in preventing domestic violence, reducing evictions, and improving the well-being and promoting the interests of all individuals and families (Whittaker 2018).

Do young people's rights have cross-national consequences?

Does the advancement of young people's rights in one country have consequences for other countries? While a strong causal relationship cannot be identified, evidence indicates that young people's rights do have cross-national consequences. A clear instance is visible in the ratification of the UN Convention. As you know, the UN Convention is the most ratified of all UN treaties. While evidence of decoupling of commitments to the UN Convention from national practices is widely found, most national governments file reports to and appear before the UN Committee to describe their efforts at implementing the UN Convention.

The establishment of independent children's rights institutions demonstrates that young people's rights do have cross-national consequences. Having started in Scandinavian countries, such as Norway, and later established itself in western European countries like Belgium, independent children's rights institutions are presently based in Africa, Asia, eastern Europe, the Middle East and North Africa, Oceania, and the Americas, as well as other western European countries. Although the offices have different qualities, ranging from their budgets to staff size, nearly all are endowed with legal powers to serve missions of monitoring and advancing rights of young people living in their countries.

We have examined bans of corporal punishment of young people. The organization End Corporal Punishment has provided research indicating that bans of corporal punishment of young people have been implemented, affecting schools and juvenile detention facilities. Bans of corporal punishment in family homes have been slower, yet a recent report from End Corporal Punishment indicates that more and more societies are prohibiting corporal punishment in all domains where young people live (End Corporal Punishment 2020).

The World Bank has identified positive patterns in formal, primary education of young people. The optimistic trends the World Bank has identified concern access to primary education. Still, the World Bank has recently expressed concerns that young people are not learning while enrolled in formal education. A problem is data. The World Bank (2019) has made a powerful call for cross-national evidence of student performance. Without these data, we cannot be confident that students are learning, the outcome we hope the right to education fulfills. This data problem may go beyond the right to education to other entitlements young people possess.

Despite these positive trends, evidence also indicates that some change is happening slowly, if at all. A clear example concerns political rights belonging to young people. As we have discussed, young people are typically not entitled to vote until age 18 or older, across the world. Likewise, young people are typically not entitled to run for and hold political office until age 25 or older. This failure to extend young people's voting rights is typically attributed to young people's lack of competency and education. This explanation ignores young people's capabilities and competency, as well as their best interests. Indeed, the denial of young people's right to vote ignores the crucial stakes and interests young people have in the future of their nation states and international relations.

What rights are missing?

The rights articulated in the UN Convention are treated as aspirations. As we have discussed, the UN Committee has the job of ensuring that national governments take steps to implement the Convention and its rights. This chapter has presented information about instances in which the UN Committee is cooperating with other UN committees in areas of mutual interest. These instances are limited to three General Comments, as of the time of this chapter's writing. This book has emphasized that, as humans, children are entitled to all human rights. Many rights that are articulated in other treaties are not articulated in the UN Convention on the Rights of the Child. Herein lies a weakness in the UN approach. The UN Committee is tasked with monitoring implementation of the

UN Convention. The other UN committees are tasked with monitoring implementation of their particular conventions. Given the idea that young people and their rights merit extra attention, the failure of other UN committees to consider young people's experiences and needs in implementing other UN conventions is a significant weakness in the UN approach to young people's rights.

As mentioned, the human right to science merits attention. The human right to science is articulated in the UDHR and the ICESCR. Young people stand to make significant gains from implementing their right to science, from their educations to their careers to dissemination of valuable scientific information useful to improving lives. Yet the right to science presently is the bailiwick of the UN Committee on Economic, Social and Cultural Rights. The wheels are slowly moving forward for the UN Committee to take on the task of implementing and monitoring the human right to science belonging to young people.

So what about the United States?

As of the writing of this book, the US government is the only UN member state not to have ratified the UN Convention. While a prediction of whether and when the US government will ratify the UN Convention is beyond this book and, after all, difficult to make, clear support of the UN Convention can be found among the US population.

Valuable evidence exists that the distance between US laws and practices and the UN Convention is not great. Law professor Jonathan Todres (Todres, Wojcik, and Revaz 2006) has taken the lead in providing empirical evidence that the United States would not need to take big steps to comply with the UN Convention. Among the bigger challenges Todres and colleagues identify is the United States' federal system of government, which empowers state governments to take on many responsibilities.

A superficial analysis would suggest that Americans whose political leanings are to the left are the ones who will support US ratification of the UN Convention. In fact, it was the Clinton Democrat administration that signed the UN Convention. In addition, a common assumption is that Americans whose political leanings are to the right are the ones who oppose US ratification of the UN Convention and, as is often said, any UN convention.

Figure 5.2   Ishmael Beah, former child soldier from Sierra Leone, addresses a press conference at the UN Headquarters in New York to launch a new global network of children formerly affected by war. This was made possible as a result of the Optional Protocol on Child Soldiers. (Photo: UN Photo / Eskinder Debebe)

Yet these assumptions may be misguided. It was the administration of President George W. Bush, the 43rd US President and a conservative Republican, that participated in ratification of two optional protocols to the UN Convention. In 2002, the US government ratified two optional protocols to the Convention on the Rights of the Child. One protocol deals with involvement of children in armed conflict (see figure 5.2). The second focuses on the sale of children, child prostitution, and child pornography. Predicting if and when the United States will ratify the UN Convention cannot be based on politics of US Presidents or other government officials. We cannot conclude the US electorate is hostile to children's rights. Still, as each year passes, the US failure to ratify the UNCRC seems strange and isolating.

"Time will tell" whether the US government will ratify the UN Convention.

CHAPTER 6

What Is Right with Children's Rights?

Introduction

"What's wrong with children's rights?" Why do some governments, organizations, and even experts contend that children's rights are "wrong?" What are the dangers of children's rights? Are these concerns specific to groups of young people (Freeman 2000)? Or do they pertain to specific cultural traditions?

This chapter will deliberate on impacts of these arguments for children's rights. After all, if these arguments take hold, can we say young people truly possess human rights? This chapter will examine prominent arguments made against children's rights. Following these analyses, we will conclude with a discussion of what is right with children's rights.

What is wrong with children's rights?

Professor Martin Guggenheim is a professor of Law on the faculty of New York University, where he co-directs the Law School's Family Defense Clinic. He has argued cases on children's rights for over 45 years, including groundbreaking cases on juvenile delinquency and parental rights before the US Supreme Court. In 2005, Guggenheim published his book *What's Wrong with Children's Rights?* Many students of children's rights were taken aback by his book. Guggenheim is a leading advocate of children's rights in the United States. What would worry him about young people's rights?

Guggenheim's thesis is that a movement to advance children's rights not only has failed, it may have harmed young people and their families. Guggenheim's approach is to conceptualize two separate matters when it comes to children's rights: children's rights with regards to the state, and children's rights with regards to parental authority. Guggenheim focuses on the latter: children's rights with regards to parental authority.

Guggenheim's approach is sociological. He argues that children and children's rights are social. Children and their rights do not exist in a vacuum. Rather, Guggenheim (2005: 13) asserts that "Children are inherently dependent for much of the time they remain in the category of 'child.'" Let's think through Guggenheim's ideas. As we deliberate, let's consider whether his concerns only apply to young people living in the United States, or whether they extend to all young people?

Guggenheim's study concentrates on the rights of young people in court proceedings. He (2005: xii) focuses on children's rights in regards to the state when it comes to a young person's relationship with biological and adoptive parents, as well as grandparents, divorcing and divorced parents, child welfare agencies and parents, and state officials and parents. Guggenheim is concerned with these relationships because, he contends, it is in US courts that adoption, divorce, custody and visitation, foster care, and termination of parental rights play out.

Despite calling for a broader understanding of where young people and their parents fit into a larger social perspective, Guggenheim seems to place these relationships in adversarial situations, such as child versus parent. Guggenheim (2005: 17) notes that: "Simply stated, the bulk of laws affecting children in the United States are interwoven with the laws of parental authority."

A good point, but one that reveals a limit of Guggenheim's approach. He starts his analysis with the provision that he is not considering children's relationships with the state. Yet Guggenheim's approach of distinguishing the state separately from his analysis of children's and parents' rights, out of family lives, is in many ways not possible. Although Aristotle's state may not intervene into some domains on behalf of young people and their rights, the state nonetheless shapes society and how we live together (Stevens 1999).

Guggenheim does not thoroughly consider rights of young people outside their families. This approach mirrors debates over children's rights in the United States. His approach fails to consider other aspects of young people's rights and their potential impacts on children's lives: education, health, safety, voting, and young people living without parents and family in their day-to-day lives. Guggenheim's conception ignores these important rights and their value to young people's lives.

Many US critics of the UNCRC fail to consider potential impacts of children's rights not only for children, but for their parents and community. So often in the United States, a child's right to education is framed as taking away a parent's authority over her child's education (e.g., The Justice Foundation n.d.). As you know, this concern is misplaced. Rather, the UNCRC, the dominant treaty outlining children's rights, is consistent with US practices. Article 5 of the Convention asserts that "States Parties shall respect the responsibilities, rights and duties of parents or, where applicable, the members of the extended family ... to provide ... appropriate direction and guidance in the exercise by the child of the rights recognized in the present Convention." One such right is the right to a public education, stated in Article 28. This concern of groups – sometimes called parents' rights groups – takes away attention from whether all young people in the United States enjoy rights to an appropriate public education, and what efforts are needed to ensure young people can exercise their rights to education. The US Commission on Civil Rights (2018: Letter of Transmittal), an independent, bipartisan agency that the US Congress established in 1957, reported that some US students "do not have access to high-quality schools simply because of where they live ... Low-income students and students of color are often relegated to low-quality school facilities that lack equitable access to teachers, instructional materials, technology and technology support, critical facilities, and physical maintenance." This denial of the right to a free and appropriate education is a failure to implement children's rights according to the UNCRC and to US laws.

Guggenheim is correct that we should think about how young people are dependent on others to exercise their rights. Rarely does a young person choose her school or enroll in that school. Rarely does a young person select the neighborhood in which she grows up, the safety it provides or violence it presents, the playgrounds and exercise equipment she can enjoy, or the library she can visit. Guggenheim's focus on courts and parental authority leads us to overlook important problems facing young people, their parents, and their communities, and how children's rights are necessary to overcoming these problems.

Guggenheim makes powerful points, yet the dichotomy of children's rights with regard to the family and rights with regard to the state does not help us think carefully about how rights can protect young people from harm. A focus on child–parent rights may be so narrow that we fail to consider interests of young people in domains outside the family home, including economic exploitation of young people working in hazardous conditions, denial of rights to education to people with disabilities, or violence committed against young people.

Guggenheim seems concerned with how US courts work – in particular, that rights will foment litigious activities between young people and their caretakers, especially parents. Guggenheim's discussion reminds us of the socio-legal concept "adversarial legalism." Robert A. Kagan, a political scientist, describes the notion of adversarial legalism as especially characteristic of the United States. The United States, according to Kagan (1991: 369), "is uniquely prone to adversarial, legalistic modes of policy formulation and implementation, shaped by the prospect of judicial review." Kagan (1991: 372; 2003; 2019) contends that adversarial legalism consists of "more complex legal rules; more formal, adversarial procedures for resolving political and scientific disputes; slower, more costly forms of legal contestation; stronger, more punitive legal sanctions; more frequent judicial review of and intervention into administrative decisions; and more political controversy about (and more frequent change of) legal rules and institutions." At the heart of adversarial legalism, says Kagan, are three characteristics: formal legal contestation, meaning parties deploy rights and procedures to pursue their claims; litigant activism, meaning legal parties significantly shape proceedings; and substantive legal uncertainty, meaning "official decisions are variable, unpredictable, and reversible." These characteristics of the US legal system trouble Guggenheim. He worries that children's rights will be deployed in a legal system that promotes conflict, activism, and uncertainty – a litigious system that will not lead to the best interests of young people. Given Kagan's notion of adversarial legalism and its application to the United States, Guggenheim may be right to worry.

While Guggenheim does not tangle with these particular characteristics of adversarial legalism, he does assert that courts should not be the place where the best interests of children are decided when parents are fighting with each other. Increasingly, legal systems around the world are taking seriously the concerns Guggenheim and Kagan have raised when it comes to children's interests and well-being. Starting in the US state of Alabama, followed by Iceland, Cyprus, and other countries, organizations are setting up offices young people can visit after experiencing trauma. In the United States, these offices are known as Child Advocacy Centers, and in some European countries, such as Iceland, they are called Barnahus, or Children's House as in Cyprus. These offices offer safe environments to young people where they may receive medical care and therapy as appropriate. On staff are counselors, social workers, and medical providers, including pediatricians. These resources are available to reduce the stress of young people in cases of domestic violence. These offices also offer an environment in which a young person can discuss experiences of trauma, such as violence, with a case worker. This discussion can be used as court testimony, thereby relieving the child of having to testify in court.

While we may discount adversarial legalism for children's rights, Kagan's ideas point to how socio-legal structures may shape cultural practices, experiences, and opinions people have, including young people. Rights and their implementation may vary according to cultural practices and traditions.

Relativism

Earlier, we discussed the foundations of children's rights. Our examination revealed that the roots of children's rights can be traced to major religions and philosophical traditions, from Islam to Confucianism, from Judeo-Christian beliefs to ancient Greek philosophy. Yet a strong, apparently durable argument against children's rights, which is also used against human rights, is that they do not apply everywhere. Some opponents to children's rights make arguments that rights do not make sense for their society's culture. This sort of argument complains about the content of children's rights and denies their utility in various societies.

Wait. All but one UN member state has ratified the UNCRC. How can we take seriously an argument based on relativism? In the big picture, the UNCRC is a relatively young document, adopted in 1989, barely 30 years ago. The UNCRC is a widely accepted treaty, the most ratified UN human rights treaty. Does the question of relativism apply to particular rights, or particular cultures? Let's consider each.

Some scholars call this debate the Relativism–Universalism problem. Jack Donnelly (2013), a social scientist whose scholarship has prompted important research on human rights, says that cultural relativism is an undeniable fact. What he means is that "moral rules and social institutions evidence an astonishing cultural and historical variability." What Donnelly has in mind is that, even when a national government ratifies the UNCRC – the same UNCRC other national governments ratify – leadership of that government and members of that government's society may have different understandings of what the Convention says, means, and demands.

Donnelly (1984), one of the most insightful experts on human rights, identifies a range of types of relativism–universalism when it comes to human rights. Donnelly's range includes radical cultural relativism at one end, and radical universalism at the other end. Radical cultural relativism, according to Donnelly, says that culture is the only source of validity for a moral right or rule. On the other hand, radical universalism says that moral rights and rules are universally valid. Culture does not matter to the validity of a moral right or rule.

Between these ends is strong cultural relativism and weak cultural relativism (see figure 6.1). Strong cultural relativism presumes that rights are culturally determined, but some rights are universal and serve "as a check on the potential excesses of relativism" (Donnelly 1984: 401). Weak cultural relativism, on the other hand, takes the perspective that a set of universal human rights do exist, and cultural variations in those rights are "rare and strictly limited."

Figure 6.1   Despite the UNCRC and its General Comments, child imprisonment is a matter of cultural relativism. Child welfare groups report that thousands of children are locked up in police stations, detention centers, and even adult jails across the Philippines. (Photo: Preda Foundation, www.preda.org)

What is the right answer? Donnelly asserts that strong cultural relativism is a difficult argument to make. He reminds us that, when we think of rights, we are often anticipating their violation. A key concern when rights are violated is that dignity is violated. Consequently, Donnelly (1984: 417) argues that to "overcome" universality of a right, one must "demonstrate either that the anticipated violation is not standard in that society, that the value is (justifiably) not considered basic in that society, or that it is protected by an alternative mechanism." Donnelly (1984: 417) concludes that these standards are rarely met today in any society.

Reservations to the UNCRC may be understood as instances of national governments indicating what's culturally wrong with children's rights. Bearing in mind that all but one UN member party has ratified the UNCRC (as you know, the United States), these reservations, especially multiple reservations to the same article, may suggest resistance to some kinds of children's rights. Few reservations, however, have been made.

Rhoda Howard, to whom Donnelly refers, proposes the option of national legislation that would enable individuals to opt out of particular cultural activities. In her study, she proposes that women should be able to opt out of traditional practices of child marriage, for instance (Howard-Hassmann 2000).

Relativism seems to be based on the idea that individuals can sort out their preferences when it comes to societal traditions and rights. People do live in societies whose cultural traditions conflict with human rights. In these societies, rights are culturally determined in such a way that we can say they conflict with clear meanings of those rights. Let's consider these ideas on relativism for children's rights through examination of a particular right, and rights belonging to members of a social group, people who have disabilities. This comparison is meant to elucidate ideas and the meaning of relativism for children's rights, including the idea of opting out (see figure 6.1).

A clear-cut violation of children's rights is capital punishment. All UN member parties that ratified the UNCRC have agreed to prohibit this practice. Only one member party filed a reservation to the UNCRC that rejects Article 37 (a), which states:

> States Parties shall ensure that:
> (a) No child shall be subjected to torture or other cruel, inhuman or degrading treatment or punishment. Neither capital punishment nor life imprisonment without possibility of release shall be imposed for offences committed by persons below eighteen years of age.

This country was the Netherlands, which indicated its intention to apply penal law to individuals aged 16 and older. In 1860, the Netherlands abolished the death penalty. Even the United States prohibits capital punishment of young people. In 2005, the US Supreme Court published its opinion of the case *Roper v. Simmons*, which was that the US Constitution forbids execution of individuals who were under the age of 18 when they committed the crime. The majority opinion that Justice Anthony Kennedy wrote for the Court explicitly refers to the UNCRC and its prohibition of capital punishment of young people. Justice Kennedy goes on to note: "It is proper that we acknowledge the overwhelming weight of international opinion against the juvenile death penalty." With US prohibition of capital punishment of young people, we can reasonably conclude that a universal consensus among UN member parties exists.

Yet 9 countries imposed death as punishment of young people during the period 1990 to 2018. The Democratic

Republic of the Congo killed 1 young person (aged 14), Nigeria killed 1 young person (aged 15), China killed 2 young people (aged 17 and 18), Pakistan killed 9 young people (aged 13 through 17), Saudi Arabia killed 8 young people (aged 15 through 17), South Sudan killed 3 young people (under age 18; no other information available), Sudan killed 2 (aged 16 and 17), and Yemen killed 3 (aged 13 through 18). Iran killed 95 young people (aged 12 through 18). All of these countries have ratified the UNCRC. None has explicitly indicated they disavow paragraph (a) of Article 37.

Donnelly advocates for application of weak cultural relativism, the universality of basic human rights that permits limited cultural variations. He contends that to "overcome" universality of a right, an individual must show that the value inherent in that right is not accepted in that society. This contention is difficult to apply to capital punishment of young people. A child's right to be free from capital punishment clearly is a key right that protects a young person's dignity. While the distinction between basic and non-basic rights undermines a key component of children's rights, if such a distinction exists, freedom from capital punishment would probably be an instance of a basic children's right. Cultural variation when it comes to capital punishment does not seem acceptable given its universal rejection, as well as its inherent denial of human dignity. In sum, capital punishment of young people is a clear violation of children's rights. Governments that impose death on young people are in clear violation of the UNCRC, an international law they have agreed to implement domestically. Application of weak cultural relativism to freedom from capital punishment is hard to imagine, if not impossible.

The rights of people with disabilities have received greater attention in the last 20 years. Referring to discriminatory practices experienced by people with disabilities, UN Deputy

Secretary-General Amina J. Mohammed asserted that this situation "goes against our collective commitment to human dignity, our obligations under international law and the strong business case for disability inclusion." This attention especially is true of young people, according to the Deputy Secretary-General. In 2006, the United Nations adopted the Convention on the Rights of People with Disabilities (CRPD). As of 2020, over 180 UN members have ratified and 10 have signed the Convention, with only 8 not yet taking action. These ratifications indicate commitments to the rights of people with disabilities, including young people.

In the same year that the UN adopted the CRPD, the UN Committee on the Rights of the Child published General Comment no. 9, "The rights of children with disabilities." Through this General Comment, the UN Committee notes the large number of children in the world who have disabilities, and that these young people are encountering difficulties in, and barriers to, exercising their rights. The Committee emphasizes that these barriers are not due to disabilities, but obstacles young people encounter in the societies in which they live and grow up. The Committee calls on UN member parties to remove these obstacles.

Nevertheless, the World Policy Analysis Center reports ongoing, significant discrimination against young people who have disabilities (World Policy Analysis Center n.d.). The Center finds that only 28% of the 193 countries they examined articulate in their constitutions the right to education for children who have disabilities. Among low- and middle-income countries, their analyses indicate that children who have disabilities are 30 to 50 percentage points less enrolled in school.

Experts have uncovered cultural practices that violate rights of people with disabilities, including rights of young people.

Human Rights Watch (HRW) has documented harsh practices that violate rights of individuals who have disabilities. In Nigeria, people who have mental health disabilities may be chained, even shackled (Human Rights Watch 2010). HRW (2018) finds that Lebanese public schools have denied admission to children who have disabilities. Jordan, HRW concludes, has failed to allocate appropriate funds to education of children with disabilities, and segregates education of these young people. Is it reasonable to assume that these cultural practices are acceptable to people with disabilities?

Do we really have to ask? Or is it reasonable to expect that people with disabilities possess rights to health and health care, to education, to avoiding discrimination, and that the societies in which they live should empower exercise of these rights? A question we can pose is whether these cultural practices that violate rights of people with disabilities are acceptable.

These issues are particularly challenging for young people. If a society's cultural practices include violating rights of young people who have disabilities, do we accept those practices? Across the world, adults, even parents, may fail to ensure that rights of young people who have disabilities are implemented. Worse, they may violate those rights. If a young person must rely on an adult to be able to exercise rights, and a cultural belief and practice are to violate the rights of that young person, do we accept it? Another way to say it is: is it acceptable to turn our backs on young people who have disabilities?

Relativism is a hard perspective to accept when it comes to rights of people, including children, with disabilities. The UN, HRW, and other organizations have documented violations of a range of rights that everyone possesses, but these violations are imposed on people with disabilities. These violations undermine the dignity of everyone. Weak cultural relativism is difficult to apply to violations of rights of children who have disabilities. Rights to education, to freedom of movement, and to bodily control, all can be considered basic rights whose values are ignored when they are violated.

It may be reasonable to expect adults can sort, then opt out of, cultural practices in their societies, so they can exercise their rights. It is hard to imagine, however, a young person opting out of a cultural tradition in pursuit of implementation of a children's right. Opting out of cultural traditions of discrimination seems especially difficult when the person who wants to exercise rights is a young person. This point is important because it reflects on both cultural relativism and children's rights.

A cultural tradition that continues to be found in many societies is physical punishment of young people. The organization End Corporal Punishment has established the goal of a global ban on physical punishment of children (End Corporal Punishment 2020). In the meantime, End Corporal Punishment has encountered resistance to its efforts. One challenge to the organization's efforts is the argument that parents possess a right to use physical punishment as a means of disciplining their children. To assert that parents have the right to act violently against their children reveals dubious ideas that serve as foundations to some groups' notions of parents' rights. This argument suggests that parents enjoy a status that is legally extraordinary. In most societies, committing an assault is illegal. The argument that parents possess a right to punish a child physically suggests that some groups have the mistaken belief that parents are beyond the law. Surely the answer to this question is that parents cannot commit illegal acts just because they are parents.

Infamous situations of child abuse elucidate this problem, as well as highlight the vulnerability of young people and their reliance on adults to implement their rights. One such situation is seen in the well-known 1989 US Supreme Court case, *Deshaney v. Winnebago County Department of Social Services* (489 US 189). Joshua Deshaney was a 4-year-old boy when his father violently harmed him over a sustained period of time. The injuries led to Joshua experiencing brain damage from which he would not recover. The Winnebago County Department of Social Services was responsible for monitoring Joshua's well-being, yet allowed the boy to remain in his father's custody despite documented evidence of beatings. In fact, in court, a County Department employee testified: "I just knew the phone would ring some day and Joshua would be dead." Joshua's mother sued the County Department, accusing it of failing to follow procedures, which then led to denying her son protections that would have saved him from his father's violence and the injuries he sustained. Surprisingly, the US Supreme Court ruled that Joshua was not denied due process and did not have rights to protection from the County Department.

The *Deshaney* lawsuit is, in many ways, a worst-case scenario. A child is abused by his parent, a person who is supposed to protect and nurture him. Government employees who are supposed to protect the child from harm and ensure that the child goes to school, receives health care when needed, and grows up in a safe and secure environment fail this child. These employees even recognize that their failures may lead to the child's death. A legal system that is there to ensure a child's rights are enforced when a person physically harms this child fails so badly that the child never recovers and loses the chance to go to school and to enjoy a healthy life. The highest court in the United States ultimately decides the child is marginal and vulnerable. This child does not deserve protections that only adults can provide. Yet this worst-case scenario is not unusual

(Chemerinsky 2007). The US Supreme Court confirmed its decision that due process was not denied in similar cases. Similar scenarios have occurred in other countries, such as the Victoria Climbié inquiry in the United Kingdom, a situation where a girl repeatedly fell through the cracks of government social services, and died after torture and abuse that led to her death at 8 years old. Not only were young people in these horrible situations unable to "opt out," but also the people on whom they relied to exercise their rights failed to do so, and some were the ones who violated the child's rights terribly.

When it comes to children's rights, arguments based on relativism seem misplaced, even empty. On the one hand, the UNCRC has been ratified by every UN member party except one: the United States. Even the United States has ratified two optional protocols to the UNCRC, and its Supreme Court has referred to the UNCRC in making its decisions. On the other hand, the framework proposed around relativism seems to suggest that, if a right is contrary to a cultural tradition, a person should opt out and exercise her rights. Our discussion of freedom from capital punishment, rights of young people with disabilities, and traditions of physical punishment of young people suggest that the concept of opting out may be impracticable for young people.

Indeed, these three scenarios highlight Guggenheim's concern that young people typically rely on adults to help exercise their rights. They point to a problem with Guggenheim's thinking, which is that children's interests can diverge from the interests of adults, including the child's parents.

What is right about children's rights?

The Preamble to the UN Convention on the Rights of the Child offers insights into what is right with children's rights.

The Preamble points to human rights principles articulated in other human rights treaties, notably the ICCPR and the ICESCR. The Preamble then proceeds to assert reasons why we need the UNCRC.

The Preamble states that all people possess inherent dignity and equality. The Preamble is clear that these qualities of dignity and equality apply to everyone, all members of humanity. This membership is part of being human, no matter the societies in which we live. While T. H. Marshall calls for establishing societal membership through citizenship rights, the UN is calling for membership in humanity. All people possess this membership.

The Preamble to the UNCRC proceeds to articulate why children's rights are needed in addition to human rights. Referring to the 1959 Declaration of the Rights of the Child, the UN says children need their own set of rights to provide safeguards and protections: "Bearing in mind that, as indicated in the Declaration of the Rights of the Child, 'the child, by reason of his physical and mental immaturity, needs special safeguards and care, including appropriate legal protection, before as well as after birth.'"

Do children's rights provide safeguards and protections? Certainly. A freedom of conscience allows a young person to think on her own and to make her own decisions, including decisions on how to exercise rights. A right to assemble empowers a young person to join a group of like-minded people. Such a group may enable young people to work together to produce social change, including winning the right to vote. A right of education is essential to knowledge for knowledge's sake. A right to education can help a person obtain and digest information that will make them a more effective voter and consumer. A right to education can help a young person exercise her freedoms from hazardous work and economic exploitation.

Are these safeguards enough? Probably not. Guggenheim is right that young people rely on adults. This reliance occurs not only due to young people's age and physical and emotional needs, but due to structures we have created, such as competency rules, age-based qualifications, and age-based prohibitions. While the UNCRC should be understood as a minimal floor, not a ceiling of aspiration, we should keep in mind that children do not live by rights alone. The UNCRC was never meant to be the sole mechanism for ensuring better lives and futures for young people. Like everyone, young people need families, nourishment and security, love and independence. Children's rights may be keys to societal membership. Young people should be embraced by societies that value their inherent dignity. Young people should be considered participants whose views are understood, valued, and considered equally with other societal members. Societies should take children and their rights seriously.

Sociology of children's rights

A sociological approach to studying children's rights reveals not only many aspects of these rights, but that children's rights are a window into how we think about human rights. Why are children's rights needed? Human rights are supposed to reduce marginality; human rights are supposed to prevent vulnerability; human rights are supposed to be universal. If human rights are meaningful and effective, why do we need children's rights? A conclusion we can draw, which apparently is the same conclusion the UN has reached, is that human rights fail young people. This conclusion is more than disappointing. Insisting that human rights work for young people would suggest that young people are the same as everyone. They are human and members of society. Insisting on children's rights suggests young people do not enjoy societal membership. Because human rights are supposed to reduce marginality, they should ensure that young people are members of mainstream society.

A sociological approach to studying children's rights reveals how societies "do," and do not do, young people's rights, and how young people experience those rights. A sociological approach identifies structures and organizations that can facilitate children's rights, as well as how rules and offices are obstacles. As you know, the UN Committee on the Rights of the Child is responsible for monitoring national governments' efforts to implement the UN Convention. The Committee's 18 independent experts are responsible for monitoring children's rights all over the world – a monumental task. Since 2014, the UN Committee has been able to hear individual complaints of young people about their rights. While this individual complaint procedure is relatively new and is organized around rules that make the procedure challenging to use, it is a new means of monitoring young people's lives and well-being. This procedure presents another significant undertaking for the UN Committee. Independent children's rights institutions have been established to monitor their governments' efforts to implement the UNCRC and advance children's rights. Many of these offices are under-staffed and under-funded. Their work is cut out for them. The work of the UN Committee, independent children's rights institutions, and the work of many national governments to ensure young people can exercise rights to which they are entitled, may lead to social change that ensures young people are living childhoods that are safe, healthy, and happy – that prepare them to become members of societies where, as adults, they are safe, healthy, and happy.

Over the course of this book, we have found evidence that young people are kept at the margins of society. They are legally prohibited from politics, neither able to vote nor to run for office. Societies are organized in ways that force young people to depend on adults. Adults have set up institutions and rules that keep young people on the margins in other ways. Young people cannot exercise many – if any – of their rights without others' support, a fact with which most adults do not have to deal. This arrangement of rights for young people can exacerbate a child's marginality and vulnerability when the young person is legally attached to an adult who does not have the access or ability to ensure her own rights can be implemented. This predicament is made worse in societies that do not consider young people's welfare to be a societal responsibility.

Our study does offer hope that children's rights may change the world. Children's rights can be and have been used to demand social change. Even in the United States, children's rights are a source of inspiration for Supreme Court justices deciding to prohibit capital punishment of young people. Children's rights can be and have been used to call on adults to take seriously rights to meaningful and equitable education, safety and security, and improving family relationships. Children's rights can be and have been used to call for improved environmental practices (United Nations General Assembly 2018). Young people are smart to employ their rights to protect environments adults are destroying – the very environments in which young people will live long after parents and political leaders are gone.

Appendices

Article 1
For the purposes of the present Convention, a child means every human being below the age of eighteen years unless under the law applicable to the child, majority is attained earlier.

Article 2
1. States Parties shall respect and ensure the rights set forth in the present Convention to each child within their jurisdiction without discrimination of any kind, irrespective of the child's or his or her parent's or legal guardian's race, colour, sex, language, religion, political or other opinion, national, ethnic or social origin, property, disability, birth or other status.

2. States Parties shall take all appropriate measures to ensure that the child is protected against all forms of discrimination or punishment on the basis of the status, activities, expressed opinions, or beliefs of the child's parents, legal guardians, or family members.

Article 3
1. In all actions concerning children, whether undertaken by public or private social welfare institutions, courts of law, administrative authorities or legislative bodies, the best interests of the child shall be a primary consideration.

2. States Parties undertake to ensure the child such protection and care as is necessary for his or her well-being, taking into account the rights and duties of his or her parents, legal guardians, or other

individuals legally responsible for him or her, and, to this end, shall take all appropriate legislative and administrative measures.

3. States Parties shall ensure that the institutions, services and facilities responsible for the care or protection of children shall conform with the standards established by competent authorities, particularly in the areas of safety, health, in the number and suitability of their staff, as well as competent supervision.

Article 4
States Parties shall undertake all appropriate legislative, administrative, and other measures for the implementation of the rights recognized in the present Convention. With regard to economic, social and cultural rights, States Parties shall undertake such measures to the maximum extent of their available resources and, where needed, within the framework of international co-operation.

Article 5
States Parties shall respect the responsibilities, rights and duties of parents or, where applicable, the members of the extended family or community as provided for by local custom, legal guardians or other persons legally responsible for the child, to provide, in a manner consistent with the evolving capacities of the child, appropriate direction and guidance in the exercise by the child of the rights recognized in the present Convention.

Article 6
1. States Parties recognize that every child has the inherent right to life.

2. States Parties shall ensure to the maximum extent possible the survival and development of the child.

Article 7
1. The child shall be registered immediately after birth and shall have the right from birth to a name, the right to acquire a nationality and, as far as possible, the right to know and be cared for by his or her parents.

2. States Parties shall ensure the implementation of these rights in accordance with their national law and their obligations under the

relevant international instruments in this field, in particular where the child would otherwise be stateless.

Article 8

1. States Parties undertake to respect the right of the child to preserve his or her identity, including nationality, name and family relations as recognized by law without unlawful interference.

2. Where a child is illegally deprived of some or all of the elements of his or her identity, States Parties shall provide appropriate assistance and protection, with a view to re-establishing speedily his or her identity.

Article 9

1. States Parties shall ensure that a child shall not be separated from his or her parents against their will, except when competent authorities subject to judicial review determine, in accordance with applicable law and procedures, that such separation is necessary for the best interests of the child. Such determination may be necessary in a particular case such as one involving abuse or neglect of the child by the parents, or one where the parents are living separately and a decision must be made as to the child's place of residence.

2. In any proceedings pursuant to paragraph 1 of the present article, all interested parties shall be given an opportunity to participate in the proceedings and make their views known.

3. States Parties shall respect the right of the child who is separated from one or both parents to maintain personal relations and direct contact with both parents on a regular basis, except if it is contrary to the child's best interests.

4. Where such separation results from any action initiated by a State Party, such as the detention, imprisonment, exile, deportation or death (including death arising from any cause while the person is in the custody of the State) of one or both parents or of the child, that State Party shall, upon request, provide the parents, the child or, if appropriate, another member of the family with the essential information concerning the whereabouts of the absent member(s) of the family unless the provision of the information would be

detrimental to the well-being of the child. States Parties shall further ensure that the submission of such a request shall of itself entail no adverse consequences for the person(s) concerned.

Article 10
1. In accordance with the obligation of States Parties under article 9, paragraph 1, applications by a child or his or her parents to enter or leave a State Party for the purpose of family reunification shall be dealt with by States Parties in a positive, humane and expeditious manner. States Parties shall further ensure that the submission of such a request shall entail no adverse consequences for the applicants and for the members of their family.

2. A child whose parents reside in different States shall have the right to maintain on a regular basis, save in exceptional circumstances personal relations and direct contacts with both parents. Towards that end and in accordance with the obligation of States Parties under article 9, paragraph 1, States Parties shall respect the right of the child and his or her parents to leave any country, including their own, and to enter their own country. The right to leave any country shall be subject only to such restrictions as are prescribed by law and which are necessary to protect the national security, public order (ordre public), public health or morals or the rights and freedoms of others and are consistent with the other rights recognized in the present Convention.

Article 11
1. States Parties shall take measures to combat the illicit transfer and non-return of children abroad.

2. To this end, States Parties shall promote the conclusion of bilateral or multilateral agreements or accession to existing agreements.

Article 12
1. States Parties shall assure to the child who is capable of forming his or her own views the right to express those views freely in all matters affecting the child, the views of the child being given due weight in accordance with the age and maturity of the child.

2. For this purpose, the child shall in particular be provided the

opportunity to be heard in any judicial and administrative proceedings affecting the child, either directly, or through a representative or an appropriate body, in a manner consistent with the procedural rules of national law.

Article 13

1. The child shall have the right to freedom of expression; this right shall include freedom to seek, receive and impart information and ideas of all kinds, regardless of frontiers, either orally, in writing or in print, in the form of art, or through any other media of the child's choice.

2. The exercise of this right may be subject to certain restrictions, but these shall only be such as are provided by law and are necessary:

(a) For respect of the rights or reputations of others; or

(b) For the protection of national security or of public order (ordre public), or of public health or morals.

Article 14

1. States Parties shall respect the right of the child to freedom of thought, conscience and religion.

2. States Parties shall respect the rights and duties of the parents and, when applicable, legal guardians, to provide direction to the child in the exercise of his or her right in a manner consistent with the evolving capacities of the child.

3. Freedom to manifest one's religion or beliefs may be subject only to such limitations as are prescribed by law and are necessary to protect public safety, order, health or morals, or the fundamental rights and freedoms of others.

Article 15

1. States Parties recognize the rights of the child to freedom of association and to freedom of peaceful assembly.

2. No restrictions may be placed on the exercise of these rights other than those imposed in conformity with the law and which are necessary in a democratic society in the interests of national security or public safety, public order (ordre public), the protection of public

health or morals or the protection of the rights and freedoms of others.

Article 16
1. No child shall be subjected to arbitrary or unlawful interference with his or her privacy, family, home or correspondence, nor to unlawful attacks on his or her honour and reputation.

2. The child has the right to the protection of the law against such interference or attacks.

Article 17
States Parties recognize the important function performed by the mass media and shall ensure that the child has access to information and material from a diversity of national and international sources, especially those aimed at the promotion of his or her social, spiritual and moral well-being and physical and mental health.

To this end, States Parties shall:

(a) Encourage the mass media to disseminate information and material of social and cultural benefit to the child and in accordance with the spirit of article 29;

(b) Encourage international co-operation in the production, exchange and dissemination of such information and material from a diversity of cultural, national and international sources;

(c) Encourage the production and dissemination of children's books;

(d) Encourage the mass media to have particular regard to the linguistic needs of the child who belongs to a minority group or who is indigenous;

(e) Encourage the development of appropriate guidelines for the protection of the child from information and material injurious to his or her well-being, bearing in mind the provisions of articles 13 and 18.

Article 18
1. States Parties shall use their best efforts to ensure recognition of the principle that both parents have common responsibilities for

the upbringing and development of the child. Parents or, as the case may be, legal guardians, have the primary responsibility for the upbringing and development of the child. The best interests of the child will be their basic concern.

2. For the purpose of guaranteeing and promoting the rights set forth in the present Convention, States Parties shall render appropriate assistance to parents and legal guardians in the performance of their child-rearing responsibilities and shall ensure the development of institutions, facilities and services for the care of children.

3. States Parties shall take all appropriate measures to ensure that children of working parents have the right to benefit from child-care services and facilities for which they are eligible.

Article 19
1. States Parties shall take all appropriate legislative, administrative, social and educational measures to protect the child from all forms of physical or mental violence, injury or abuse, neglect or negligent treatment, maltreatment or exploitation, including sexual abuse, while in the care of parent(s), legal guardian(s) or any other person who has the care of the child.

2. Such protective measures should, as appropriate, include effective procedures for the establishment of social programmes to provide necessary support for the child and for those who have the care of the child, as well as for other forms of prevention and for identification, reporting, referral, investigation, treatment and follow-up of instances of child maltreatment described heretofore, and, as appropriate, for judicial involvement.

Article 20
1. A child temporarily or permanently deprived of his or her family environment, or in whose own best interests cannot be allowed to remain in that environment, shall be entitled to special protection and assistance provided by the State.

2. States Parties shall in accordance with their national laws ensure alternative care for such a child.

3. Such care could include, inter alia, foster placement, kafalah of

Islamic law, adoption or if necessary placement in suitable institutions for the care of children. When considering solutions, due regard shall be paid to the desirability of continuity in a child's upbringing and to the child's ethnic, religious, cultural and linguistic background.

Article 21

States Parties that recognize and/or permit the system of adoption shall ensure that the best interests of the child shall be the paramount consideration and they shall:

(a) Ensure that the adoption of a child is authorized only by competent authorities who determine, in accordance with applicable law and procedures and on the basis of all pertinent and reliable information, that the adoption is permissible in view of the child's status concerning parents, relatives and legal guardians and that, if required, the persons concerned have given their informed consent to the adoption on the basis of such counselling as may be necessary;

(b) Recognize that inter-country adoption may be considered as an alternative means of child's care, if the child cannot be placed in a foster or an adoptive family or cannot in any suitable manner be cared for in the child's country of origin;

(c) Ensure that the child concerned by inter-country adoption enjoys safeguards and standards equivalent to those existing in the case of national adoption;

(d) Take all appropriate measures to ensure that, in inter-country adoption, the placement does not result in improper financial gain for those involved in it;

(e) Promote, where appropriate, the objectives of the present article by concluding bilateral or multilateral arrangements or agreements, and endeavour, within this framework, to ensure that the placement of the child in another country is carried out by competent authorities or organs.

Article 22

1. States Parties shall take appropriate measures to ensure that a child who is seeking refugee status or who is considered a refugee in accordance with applicable international or domestic law and

procedures shall, whether unaccompanied or accompanied by his or her parents or by any other person, receive appropriate protection and humanitarian assistance in the enjoyment of applicable rights set forth in the present Convention and in other international human rights or humanitarian instruments to which the said States are Parties.

2. For this purpose, States Parties shall provide, as they consider appropriate, co-operation in any efforts by the United Nations and other competent intergovernmental organizations or non-governmental organizations co-operating with the United Nations to protect and assist such a child and to trace the parents or other members of the family of any refugee child in order to obtain information necessary for reunification with his or her family. In cases where no parents or other members of the family can be found, the child shall be accorded the same protection as any other child permanently or temporarily deprived of his or her family environment for any reason, as set forth in the present Convention.

Article 23
1. States Parties recognize that a mentally or physically disabled child should enjoy a full and decent life, in conditions which ensure dignity, promote self-reliance and facilitate the child's active participation in the community.

2. States Parties recognize the right of the disabled child to special care and shall encourage and ensure the extension, subject to available resources, to the eligible child and those responsible for his or her care, of assistance for which application is made and which is appropriate to the child's condition and to the circumstances of the parents or others caring for the child.

3. Recognizing the special needs of a disabled child, assistance extended in accordance with paragraph 2 of the present article shall be provided free of charge, whenever possible, taking into account the financial resources of the parents or others caring for the child, and shall be designed to ensure that the disabled child has effective access to and receives education, training, health care services, rehabilitation services, preparation for employment and recreation opportunities in

a manner conducive to the child's achieving the fullest possible social integration and individual development, including his or her cultural and spiritual development.

4. States Parties shall promote, in the spirit of international cooperation, the exchange of appropriate information in the field of preventive health care and of medical, psychological and functional treatment of disabled children, including dissemination of and access to information concerning methods of rehabilitation, education and vocational services, with the aim of enabling States Parties to improve their capabilities and skills and to widen their experience in these areas. In this regard, particular account shall be taken of the needs of developing countries.

Article 24
1. States Parties recognize the right of the child to the enjoyment of the highest attainable standard of health and to facilities for the treatment of illness and rehabilitation of health. States Parties shall strive to ensure that no child is deprived of his or her right of access to such health care services.

2. States Parties shall pursue full implementation of this right and, in particular, shall take appropriate measures:

(a) To diminish infant and child mortality;

(b) To ensure the provision of necessary medical assistance and health care to all children with emphasis on the development of primary health care;

(c) To combat disease and malnutrition, including within the framework of primary health care, through, inter alia, the application of readily available technology and through the provision of adequate nutritious foods and clean drinking-water, taking into consideration the dangers and risks of environmental pollution;

(d) To ensure appropriate pre-natal and post-natal health care for mothers;

(e) To ensure that all segments of society, in particular parents and children, are informed, have access to education and are supported in the use of basic knowledge of child health and nutrition, the advantages of breastfeeding, hygiene and environmental sanitation and the prevention of accidents;

(f) To develop preventive health care, guidance for parents and family planning education and services.

3. States Parties shall take all effective and appropriate measures with a view to abolishing traditional practices prejudicial to the health of children.

4. States Parties undertake to promote and encourage international co-operation with a view to achieving progressively the full realization of the right recognized in the present article. In this regard, particular account shall be taken of the needs of developing countries.

Article 25
States Parties recognize the right of a child who has been placed by the competent authorities for the purposes of care, protection or treatment of his or her physical or mental health, to a periodic review of the treatment provided to the child and all other circumstances relevant to his or her placement.

Article 26
1. States Parties shall recognize for every child the right to benefit from social security, including social insurance, and shall take the necessary measures to achieve the full realization of this right in accordance with their national law.

2. The benefits should, where appropriate, be granted, taking into account the resources and the circumstances of the child and persons having responsibility for the maintenance of the child, as well as any other consideration relevant to an application for benefits made by or on behalf of the child.

Article 27
1. States Parties recognize the right of every child to a standard of living adequate for the child's physical, mental, spiritual, moral and social development.

2. The parent(s) or others responsible for the child have the primary responsibility to secure, within their abilities and financial capacities, the conditions of living necessary for the child's development.

3. States Parties, in accordance with national conditions and within their means, shall take appropriate measures to assist parents and others responsible for the child to implement this right and shall in case of need provide material assistance and support programmes, particularly with regard to nutrition, clothing and housing.

4. States Parties shall take all appropriate measures to secure the recovery of maintenance for the child from the parents or other persons having financial responsibility for the child, both within the State Party and from abroad. In particular, where the person having financial responsibility for the child lives in a State different from that of the child, States Parties shall promote the accession to international agreements or the conclusion of such agreements, as well as the making of other appropriate arrangements.

Article 28
1. States Parties recognize the right of the child to education, and with a view to achieving this right progressively and on the basis of equal opportunity, they shall, in particular:

(a) Make primary education compulsory and available free to all;

(b) Encourage the development of different forms of secondary education, including general and vocational education, make them available and accessible to every child, and take appropriate measures such as the introduction of free education and offering financial assistance in case of need;

(c) Make higher education accessible to all on the basis of capacity by every appropriate means;

(d) Make educational and vocational information and guidance available and accessible to all children;

(e) Take measures to encourage regular attendance at schools and the reduction of drop-out rates.

2. States Parties shall take all appropriate measures to ensure that school discipline is administered in a manner consistent with the child's human dignity and in conformity with the present Convention.

3. States Parties shall promote and encourage international cooperation in matters relating to education, in particular with a view to contributing to the elimination of ignorance and illiteracy throughout the world and facilitating access to scientific and technical knowledge and modern teaching methods. In this regard, particular account shall be taken of the needs of developing countries.

Article 29

1. States Parties agree that the education of the child shall be directed to:

(a) The development of the child's personality, talents and mental and physical abilities to their fullest potential;

(b) The development of respect for human rights and fundamental freedoms, and for the principles enshrined in the Charter of the United Nations;

(c) The development of respect for the child's parents, his or her own cultural identity, language and values, for the national values of the country in which the child is living, the country from which he or she may originate, and for civilizations different from his or her own;

(d) The preparation of the child for responsible life in a free society, in the spirit of understanding, peace, tolerance, equality of sexes, and friendship among all peoples, ethnic, national and religious groups and persons of indigenous origin;

(e) The development of respect for the natural environment.

2. No part of the present article or article 28 shall be construed so as to interfere with the liberty of individuals and bodies to establish and direct educational institutions, subject always to the observance of the principle set forth in paragraph 1 of the present article and to the requirements that the education given in such institutions shall conform to such minimum standards as may be laid down by the State.

Article 30

In those States in which ethnic, religious or linguistic minorities or persons of indigenous origin exist, a child belonging to such a minority or who is indigenous shall not be denied the right, in community with other members of his or her group, to enjoy his or her own culture, to profess and practise his or her own religion, or to use his or her own language.

Article 31

1. States Parties recognize the right of the child to rest and leisure, to engage in play and recreational activities appropriate to the age of the child and to participate freely in cultural life and the arts.

2. States Parties shall respect and promote the right of the child to participate fully in cultural and artistic life and shall encourage the provision of appropriate and equal opportunities for cultural, artistic, recreational and leisure activity.

Article 32

1. States Parties recognize the right of the child to be protected from economic exploitation and from performing any work that is likely to be hazardous or to interfere with the child's education, or to be harmful to the child's health or physical, mental, spiritual, moral or social development.

2. States Parties shall take legislative, administrative, social and educational measures to ensure the implementation of the present article. To this end, and having regard to the relevant provisions of other international instruments, States Parties shall in particular:

(a) Provide for a minimum age or minimum ages for admission to employment;

(b) Provide for appropriate regulation of the hours and conditions of employment;

(c) Provide for appropriate penalties or other sanctions to ensure the effective enforcement of the present article.

Article 33

States Parties shall take all appropriate measures, including legislative, administrative, social and educational measures, to protect children from the illicit use of narcotic drugs and psychotropic substances as defined in the relevant international treaties, and to prevent the use of children in the illicit production and trafficking of such substances.

Article 34
States Parties undertake to protect the child from all forms of sexual exploitation and sexual abuse. For these purposes, States Parties shall in particular take all appropriate national, bilateral and multilateral measures to prevent:

(a) The inducement or coercion of a child to engage in any unlawful sexual activity;

(b) The exploitative use of children in prostitution or other unlawful sexual practices;

(c) The exploitative use of children in pornographic performances and materials.

Article 35
States Parties shall take all appropriate national, bilateral and multilateral measures to prevent the abduction of, the sale of or traffic in children for any purpose or in any form.

Article 36
States Parties shall protect the child against all other forms of exploitation prejudicial to any aspects of the child's welfare.

Article 37
States Parties shall ensure that:

(a) No child shall be subjected to torture or other cruel, inhuman or degrading treatment or punishment. Neither capital punishment nor life imprisonment without possibility of release shall be imposed for offences committed by persons below eighteen years of age;

(b) No child shall be deprived of his or her liberty unlawfully or arbitrarily. The arrest, detention or imprisonment of a child shall be in conformity with the law and shall be used only as a measure of last resort and for the shortest appropriate period of time;

(c) Every child deprived of liberty shall be treated with humanity and respect for the inherent dignity of the human person, and in a manner which takes into account the needs of persons of his or her age. In particular, every child deprived of liberty shall be separated from adults unless it is considered in the child's best interest not to do so and shall have the right to maintain contact with his or her family through correspondence and visits, save in exceptional circumstances;

(d) Every child deprived of his or her liberty shall have the right to prompt access to legal and other appropriate assistance, as well as the right to challenge the legality of the deprivation of his or her liberty before a court or other competent, independent and impartial authority, and to a prompt decision on any such action.

Article 38
1. States Parties undertake to respect and to ensure respect for rules of international humanitarian law applicable to them in armed conflicts which are relevant to the child.

2. States Parties shall take all feasible measures to ensure that persons who have not attained the age of fifteen years do not take a direct part in hostilities.

3. States Parties shall refrain from recruiting any person who has not attained the age of fifteen years into their armed forces. In recruiting among those persons who have attained the age of fifteen years but who have not attained the age of eighteen years, States Parties shall endeavour to give priority to those who are oldest.

4. In accordance with their obligations under international humanitarian law to protect the civilian population in armed conflicts, States Parties shall take all feasible measures to ensure protection and care of children who are affected by an armed conflict.

Article 39
States Parties shall take all appropriate measures to promote physical and psychological recovery and social reintegration of a child victim of: any form of neglect, exploitation, or abuse; torture or any other form of cruel, inhuman or degrading treatment or punishment; or

armed conflicts. Such recovery and reintegration shall take place in an environment which fosters the health, self-respect and dignity of the child.

Article 40

1. States Parties recognize the right of every child alleged as, accused of, or recognized as having infringed the penal law to be treated in a manner consistent with the promotion of the child's sense of dignity and worth, which reinforces the child's respect for the human rights and fundamental freedoms of others and which takes into account the child's age and the desirability of promoting the child's reintegration and the child's assuming a constructive role in society.

2. To this end, and having regard to the relevant provisions of international instruments, States Parties shall, in particular, ensure that:

(a) No child shall be alleged as, be accused of, or recognized as having infringed the penal law by reason of acts or omissions that were not prohibited by national or international law at the time they were committed;

(b) Every child alleged as or accused of having infringed the penal law has at least the following guarantees:

(i) To be presumed innocent until proven guilty according to law;

(ii) To be informed promptly and directly of the charges against him or her, and, if appropriate, through his or her parents or legal guardians, and to have legal or other appropriate assistance in the preparation and presentation of his or her defence;

(iii) To have the matter determined without delay by a competent, independent and impartial authority or judicial body in a fair hearing according to law, in the presence of legal or other appropriate assistance and, unless it is considered not to be in the best interest of the child, in particular, taking into account his or her age or situation, his or her parents or legal guardians;

(iv) Not to be compelled to give testimony or to confess guilt; to examine or have examined adverse witnesses and to obtain the participation and examination of witnesses on his or her behalf under conditions of equality;

(v) If considered to have infringed the penal law, to have this decision and any measures imposed in consequence thereof reviewed by a higher competent, independent and impartial authority or judicial body according to law;

(vi) To have the free assistance of an interpreter if the child cannot understand or speak the language used;

(vii) To have his or her privacy fully respected at all stages of the proceedings.

3. States Parties shall seek to promote the establishment of laws, procedures, authorities and institutions specifically applicable to children alleged as, accused of, or recognized as having infringed the penal law, and, in particular:

(a) The establishment of a minimum age below which children shall be presumed not to have the capacity to infringe the penal law;

(b) Whenever appropriate and desirable, measures for dealing with such children without resorting to judicial proceedings, providing that human rights and legal safeguards are fully respected.

4. A variety of dispositions, such as care, guidance and supervision orders; counselling; probation; foster care; education and vocational training programmes and other alternatives to institutional care shall be available to ensure that children are dealt with in a manner appropriate to their well-being and proportionate both to their circumstances and the offence.

Article 41
Nothing in the present Convention shall affect any provisions which are more conducive to the realization of the rights of the child and which may be contained in:

(a) The law of a State party; or

(b) International law in force for that State.

PART II

Article 42
States Parties undertake to make the principles and provisions of the Convention widely known, by appropriate and active means, to adults and children alike.

Article 43
1. For the purpose of examining the progress made by States Parties in achieving the realization of the obligations undertaken in the present Convention, there shall be established a Committee on the Rights of the Child, which shall carry out the functions hereinafter provided.

2. The Committee shall consist of eighteen experts of high moral standing and recognized competence in the field covered by this Convention.[1] The members of the Committee shall be elected by States Parties from among their nationals and shall serve in their personal capacity, consideration being given to equitable geographical distribution, as well as to the principal legal systems.

3. The members of the Committee shall be elected by secret ballot from a list of persons nominated by States Parties. Each State Party may nominate one person from among its own nationals.

4. The initial election to the Committee shall be held no later than six months after the date of the entry into force of the present Convention and thereafter every second year. At least four months before the date of each election, the Secretary-General of the United Nations shall address a letter to States Parties inviting them to submit their nominations within two months. The Secretary-General shall

---

[1] The General Assembly, in its resolution 50/155 of 21 December 1995, approved the amendment to article 43, paragraph 2, of the Convention on the Rights of the Child, replacing the word "ten" with the word "eighteen."
The amendment entered into force on 18 November 2002 when it had been accepted by a two-thirds majority of the States parties (128 out of 191).

subsequently prepare a list in alphabetical order of all persons thus nominated, indicating States Parties which have nominated them, and shall submit it to the States Parties to the present Convention.

5. The elections shall be held at meetings of States Parties convened by the Secretary-General at United Nations Headquarters. At those meetings, for which two thirds of States Parties shall constitute a quorum, the persons elected to the Committee shall be those who obtain the largest number of votes and an absolute majority of the votes of the representatives of States Parties present and voting.

6. The members of the Committee shall be elected for a term of four years. They shall be eligible for re-election if renominated. The term of five of the members elected at the first election shall expire at the end of two years; immediately after the first election, the names of these five members shall be chosen by lot by the Chairman of the meeting.

7. If a member of the Committee dies or resigns or declares that for any other cause he or she can no longer perform the duties of the Committee, the State Party which nominated the member shall appoint another expert from among its nationals to serve for the remainder of the term, subject to the approval of the Committee.

8. The Committee shall establish its own rules of procedure.

9. The Committee shall elect its officers for a period of two years.

10. The meetings of the Committee shall normally be held at United Nations Headquarters or at any other convenient place as determined by the Committee. The Committee shall normally meet annually. The duration of the meetings of the Committee shall be determined, and reviewed, if necessary, by a meeting of the States Parties to the present Convention, subject to the approval of the General Assembly.

11. The Secretary-General of the United Nations shall provide the necessary staff and facilities for the effective performance of the functions of the Committee under the present Convention.

12. With the approval of the General Assembly, the members of the Committee established under the present Convention shall receive

emoluments from United Nations resources on such terms and conditions as the Assembly may decide.

Article 44
1. States Parties undertake to submit to the Committee, through the Secretary-General of the United Nations, reports on the measures they have adopted which give effect to the rights recognized herein and on the progress made on the enjoyment of those rights

(a) Within two years of the entry into force of the Convention for the State Party concerned;

(b) Thereafter every five years.

2. Reports made under the present article shall indicate factors and difficulties, if any, affecting the degree of fulfilment of the obligations under the present Convention. Reports shall also contain sufficient information to provide the Committee with a comprehensive understanding of the implementation of the Convention in the country concerned.

3. A State Party which has submitted a comprehensive initial report to the Committee need not, in its subsequent reports submitted in accordance with paragraph 1 (b) of the present article, repeat basic information previously provided.

4. The Committee may request from States Parties further information relevant to the implementation of the Convention.

5. The Committee shall submit to the General Assembly, through the Economic and Social Council, every two years, reports on its activities.

6. States Parties shall make their reports widely available to the public in their own countries.

Article 45
In order to foster the effective implementation of the Convention and to encourage international co-operation in the field covered by the Convention:

(a) The specialized agencies, the United Nations Children's Fund, and other United Nations organs shall be entitled to be represented at the consideration of the implementation of such provisions of the present Convention as fall within the scope of their mandate. The Committee may invite the specialized agencies, the United Nations Children's Fund and other competent bodies as it may consider appropriate to provide expert advice on the implementation of the Convention in areas falling within the scope of their respective mandates. The Committee may invite the specialized agencies, the United Nations Children's Fund, and other United Nations organs to submit reports on the implementation of the Convention in areas falling within the scope of their activities;

(b) The Committee shall transmit, as it may consider appropriate, to the specialized agencies, the United Nations Children's Fund and other competent bodies, any reports from States Parties that contain a request, or indicate a need, for technical advice or assistance, along with the Committee's observations and suggestions, if any, on these requests or indications;

(c) The Committee may recommend to the General Assembly to request the Secretary-General to undertake on its behalf studies on specific issues relating to the rights of the child;

(d) The Committee may make suggestions and general recommendations based on information received pursuant to articles 44 and 45 of the present Convention. Such suggestions and general recommendations shall be transmitted to any State Party concerned and reported to the General Assembly, together with comments, if any, from States Parties.

PART III

Article 46
The present Convention shall be open for signature by all States.

Article 47
The present Convention is subject to ratification. Instruments of ratification shall be deposited with the Secretary-General of the United Nations.

Article 48
The present Convention shall remain open for accession by any State. The instruments of accession shall be deposited with the Secretary-General of the United Nations.

Article 49
1. The present Convention shall enter into force on the thirtieth day following the date of deposit with the Secretary-General of the United Nations of the twentieth instrument of ratification or accession.

2. For each State ratifying or acceding to the Convention after the deposit of the twentieth instrument of ratification or accession, the Convention shall enter into force on the thirtieth day after the deposit by such State of its instrument of ratification or accession.

Article 50
1. Any State Party may propose an amendment and file it with the Secretary-General of the United Nations. The Secretary-General shall thereupon communicate the proposed amendment to States Parties, with a request that they indicate whether they favour a conference of States Parties for the purpose of considering and voting upon the proposals. In the event that, within four months from the date of such communication, at least one third of the States Parties favour such a conference, the Secretary-General shall convene the conference under the auspices of the United Nations. Any amendment adopted by a majority of States Parties present and voting at the conference shall be submitted to the General Assembly for approval.

2. An amendment adopted in accordance with paragraph 1 of the present article shall enter into force when it has been approved by the General Assembly of the United Nations and accepted by a two-thirds majority of States Parties.

3. When an amendment enters into force, it shall be binding on those States Parties which have accepted it, other States Parties still being bound by the provisions of the present Convention and any earlier amendments which they have accepted.

Article 51
1. The Secretary-General of the United Nations shall receive and

circulate to all States the text of reservations made by States at the time of ratification or accession.

2. A reservation incompatible with the object and purpose of the present Convention shall not be permitted.

3. Reservations may be withdrawn at any time by notification to that effect addressed to the Secretary-General of the United Nations, who shall then inform all States. Such notification shall take effect on the date on which it is received by the Secretary-General.

Article 52
A State Party may denounce the present Convention by written notification to the Secretary-General of the United Nations. Denunciation becomes effective one year after the date of receipt of the notification by the Secretary-General.

Article 53
The Secretary-General of the United Nations is designated as the depositary of the present Convention.

Article 54
The original of the present Convention, of which the Arabic, Chinese, English, French, Russian and Spanish texts are equally authentic, shall be deposited with the Secretary-General of the United Nations. In witness thereof the undersigned plenipotentiaries, being duly authorized thereto by their respective Governments, have signed the present Convention.

APPENDIX 2 FULL TABLE 5.2

Full Table 5.2 Government expenditure per student, primary education, by % of GDP per capita (World Bank 2020)

Country	Year	%	Country	Year	%
Afghanistan	2017	10.3	Cameroon	2012	5.4
Albania	2017	34.2	Canada	2015	17.6
Algeria	2003	11.5	Central African Republic	2010	4.1
Andorra	2018	12.3	Chad	2012	6.3
Angola			Chile	2017	18.4
Antigua and Barbuda	2009	8.1	China	1998	5.9
Argentina	2017	15	Colombia	2018	17
Armenia	2017	10.2	Comoros	2014	9.8
Aruba	2014	17.1	Congo, Dem. Rep.	2013	7.2
Australia	2016	19.3	Congo, Rep.	2010	11.7
Austria	2016	23.5	Costa Rica	2018	20.8
Azerbaijan			Cote d'Ivoire	2018	13.3
Bahamas			Croatia		
Bahrain	2015	11.2	Cuba	2010	49.1
Bangladesh	2009	7.6	Curacao	2013	10
Barbados	2016	20.8	Cyprus	2016	31.9
Belarus			Czech Republic	2016	13.9
Belgium	2016	21.9	Denmark	2014	25.1
Belize	2017	16.6	Djibouti	2016	37.3
Benin	2015	10.3	Dominica	2015	14.6
Bermuda	2015	8.1	Dominican Republic	2018	16.2
Bhutan	2014	12.8	Ecuador	2016	9.5
Bolivia			Egypt, Arab Rep.	2017	9.8
Bosnia and Herzegovina			El Salvador	2018	16.1
Botswana	2009	10.1	Equatorial Guinea		
Brazil	2015	20.1	Eritrea	2004	5.3
British Virgin Islands	2017	6.2	Estonia	2016	20.3
Brunei Darussalam	2016	8.9	Eswatini	2014	16.5
Bulgaria	2013	23	Ethiopia	2015	7.9
Burkina Faso	2015	16.1	Fiji	2013	12.4
Burundi	2013	12.9	Finland	2016	21.5
Cabo Verde	2017	16.7	France	2016	17.4
Cambodia	2014	6.6	Gabon	2011	4.7

Country	Year	%	Country	Year	%
Gambia, The	2015	8.5	Lao PDR	2014	9.1
Georgia	2012	8.8	Latvia	2016	24.5
Germany	2016	17.4	Lebanon		
Ghana	2014	6.4	Lesotho	2018	20.7
Gibraltar			Liberia	2016	14.5
Greece	2016	20.3	Libya		
Greenland			Liechtenstein	2011	17.8
Grenada	2017	8.2	Lithuania	2016	19.5
Guam			Luxembourg	2015	19.7
Guatemala	2018	11.9	Macao SAR, China	2003	7.6
Guinea	2016	6.8	Madagascar	2012	6.6
Guinea-Bissau	2010	4.7	Malawi	2016	8.2
Guyana	2012	7.8	Malaysia	2017	16.1
Haiti			Maldives	2016	16.1
Honduras	2013	21.4	Mali	2017	12.3
Hong Kong SAR, China	2018	14.8	Malta	2015	22.8
Hungary	2016	19.1	Marshall Islands	2002	23.6
Iceland	2016	22.1	Mauritania	2016	10.2
India	2013	9.8	Mauritius	2018	15.6
Indonesia	2015	13.3	Mexico	2016	13.8
Iran, Islamic Rep.	2017	11.1	Moldova	2018	32.5
Iraq			Monaco	2016	3.3
Ireland	2016	11.8	Mongolia	2017	14.1
Israel	2016	21.5	Montenegro		
Italy	2016	19.5	Morocco	2013	19.5
Jamaica	2018	21.7	Mozambique	2013	14.7
Japan	2016	21.8	Myanmar	2018	7.8
Jordan	2018	13.3	Namibia	2010	17.1
Kazakhstan	2018	0.2	Nauru		
Kenya	2015	11	Nepal	2015	12.4
Kiribati	2001	22.5	Netherlands	2016	16.7
Korea, Dem. People's Rep. (North Korea)			New Zealand	2016	20.3
Korea, Rep. (South Korea)	2016	27.8	Nicaragua	2010	11.3
Kosovo			Niger	2017	13.3
Kuwait	2014	14.4	Nigeria		
Kyrgyz Republic			North Macedonia		

Country	Year	%	Country	Year	%
Norway	2016	21.7	St. Lucia	2018	14.7
Oman	2016	31.8	St. Vincent and the Grenadines	2018	17.5
Pakistan	2015	8.1	Sudan		
Palau			Suriname		
Panama	2011	6.3	Sweden	2016	21.7
Papua New Guinea			Switzerland	2016	24.8
Paraguay	2016	11.7	Syrian Arab Republic	2012	16.9
Peru	2018	11.2	Tajikistan		
Philippines	2008	9.1	Tanzania	2014	9.5
Poland	2016	23.1	Thailand	2013	23.3
Portugal	2015	22.5	Timor-Leste	2014	8.3
Qatar	2009	10.2	Togo	2016	16.2
Romania	2016	7.8	Tonga	2004	9.7
Russian Federation			Trinidad and Tobago	2009	15.1
Rwanda	2018	4.3	Tunisia	2008	17.4
Samoa	2016	9	Turkey	2016	13
San Marino	2011	16.1	Turkmenistan		
Sao Tome and Principe	2014	11.9	Turks and Caicos Islands	2018	5.7
Saudi Arabia	2007	17.7	Tuvalu		
Senegal	2018	10.9	Uganda	2014	5.6
Serbia	2015	43.7	Ukraine	2017	30.3
Seychelles	2016	14.2	United Arab Emirates	1998	6
Sierra Leone	2018	12.4	United Kingdom	2016	24.2
Singapore	2017	17.5	United States	2016	19.9
Slovak Republic	2016	20.8	Uruguay	2017	12.6
Slovenia	2016	23.6	Uzbekistan		
Solomon Islands			Vanuatu	2015	13.5
Somalia			Venezuela, RB	2015	17.9
South Africa	2018	17.9	Vietnam	2013	21.1
South Sudan	2016	4.6	Yemen, Rep.	2011	18.1
Spain	2016	17.1	Zambia	2017	12.9
Sri Lanka	2018	7.9	Zimbabwe	2013	14
St. Kitts and Nevis	2015	5.2			

Full Table 5.3 Low-birthweight babies by % of births (World Bank 2020)

Country	Year	%	Country	Year	%
Afghanistan			Cameroon	2006	11
Albania	2009	4	Canada	2011	6
Algeria	2006	6	Central African Republic	2010	14
Andorra			Chad	2010	20
Angola	2000	12	Chile	2011	6
Antigua and Barbuda	2011	6	China	2012	2
Argentina	2011	7	Colombia	2012	10
Armenia	2010	8	Comoros	2000	25
Aruba			Congo, Dem. Rep.	2010	10
Australia	2010	6	Congo, Rep.	2005	13
Austria	2011	7	Costa Rica	2012	7
Azerbaijan	2006	10	Cote d'Ivoire	2006	17
Bahamas, The	2011	12	Croatia	2011	5
Bahrain	2012	10	Cuba	2012	5
Bangladesh	2006	22	Curacao		
Barbados	2011	12	Cyprus	2007	12
Belarus	2011	5	Czech Republic	2012	8
Belgium	2009	7	Denmark	2012	5
Belize	2011	11	Djibouti	2006	10
Benin	2006	15	Dominica	2011	11
Bermuda			Dominican Republic	2007	11
Bhutan	2010	10	Ecuador	2012	9
Bolivia	2008	6	Egypt, Arab Rep.	2008	13
Bosnia and Herzegovina	2012	5	El Salvador	2011	9
Botswana	2007	13	Equatorial Guinea	2000	13
Brazil	2011	9	Eritrea	2002	14
British Virgin Islands	2008	5	Estonia	2012	5
Brunei Darussalam	2011	12	Eswatini	2019	9
Bulgaria	2011	9	Ethiopia	2005	20
Burkina Faso	2010	14	Fiji	2004	10
Burundi	2010	13	Finland	2012	4
Cabo Verde	2005	6	France	2011	7
Cambodia	2010	11	French Polynesia	2000	6

Country	Year	%	Country	Year	%
Gabon	2000	14	Lao PDR	2012	15
Gambia, The	2010	10	Latvia	2012	5
Georgia	2012	7	Lebanon	2009	12
Germany	2012	7	Lesotho	2009	11
Gibraltar			Liberia	2007	14
Greece	2012	10	Libya	1995	7
Greenland			Liechtenstein		
Grenada	2011	9	Lithuania	2012	5
Guam			Luxembourg	2011	7
Guatemala	2009	11	Macao SAR, China	2000	5
Guinea	2005	12	Madagascar	2009	16
Guinea-Bissau	2010	11	Malawi	2010	14
Guyana	2009	14	Malaysia	2012	11
Haiti	2012	23	Maldives	2009	11
Honduras	2012	10	Mali	2010	18
Hong Kong SAR, China	2000	5	Malta	2011	7
Hungary	2012	9	Marshall Islands	2007	18
Iceland	2012	4	Mauritania	2011	35
India	2006	28	Mauritius	2003	14
Indonesia	2010	11	Mexico	2012	9
Iran, Islamic Rep.	2011	8	Micronesia, Fed. Sts.	2009	11
Iraq	2011	13	Moldova	2012	6
Ireland	2011	5	Monaco	2012	6
Israel	2012	19.5	Mongolia	2010	5
Italy	2010	21.7	Montenegro	2012	5
Jamaica	2011	21.8	Morocco	2004	15
Japan	2012	13.3	Mozambique	2011	17
Jordan	2007	0.2	Myanmar	2010	9
Kazakhstan	2012	11	Namibia	2007	16
Kenya	2009	22.5	Nauru	2007	27
Kiribati	2011		Nepal	2011	18
Korea, Dem. People's Rep. (North Korea)	2009	27.8	Netherlands	2010	6
Korea, Rep. (South Korea)	2006		New Caledonia	2000	8
Kosovo			New Zealand	2012	6
Kuwait	2011	8	Nicaragua	2011	8
Kyrgyz Republic	2012	6	Niger	2006	27

Country	Year	%	Country	Year	%
Nigeria	2011	15	St. Kitts and Nevis	2011	10
North Macedonia	2011	6	St. Lucia	2011	10
Norway	2009	5	St. Vincent and the Grenadines	2011	11
Oman	2012	10	Sudan	1999	31
Pakistan	2007	32	Suriname	2010	14
Palau	2010	7	Sweden	2011	5
Panama	2011	8	Switzerland	2012	7
Papua New Guinea	2005	11	Syrian Arab Republic	2009	10
Paraguay	2009	6	Tajikistan	2005	10
Peru	2011	7	Tanzania	2010	8
Philippines	2011	16	Thailand	2010	11
Poland	2012	6	Timor-Leste	2003	12
Portugal	2012	9	Togo	2010	11
Norway	2009	5	Tonga	2002	3
Qatar	2010	8	Trinidad and Tobago	2011	12
Romania	2012	8	Tunisia	2012	7
Russian Federation	2012	6	Turkey	2008	11
Rwanda	2010	7	Turkmenistan	2011	5
Samoa	2009	10	Turks and Caicos Islands	2008	7
San Marino	2011	10	Tuvalu	2007	6
Sao Tome and Principe	2009	10	Uganda	2011	12
Saudi Arabia	2012	9	Ukraine	2011	5
Senegal	2011	19	United Arab Emirates	2009	6
Serbia	2011	6	United Kingdom	2011	7
Seychelles			United States	2010	8
Sierra Leone	2010	11	Uruguay	2012	8
Singapore	2011	10	Uzbekistan	2006	5
Slovak Republic	2012	8	Vanuatu	2007	10
Slovenia	2012	6	Venezuela, RB	2011	9
Solomon Islands	2007	13	Vietnam	2011	5
Somalia			West Bank and Gaza	2010	9
South Africa	1998	15	Yemen, Rep.	2010	32
South Sudan			Zambia	2007	11
Spain	2012	8	Zimbabwe	2011	11
Sri Lanka	2007	17			

References

Abbott, E., and S. P. Breckinridge. 1917. *Truancy and Non-Attendance in the Chicago Schools*. University of Chicago Press.

Adalah, The Legal Center for Arab Minority Rights in Israel. June 23, 2013. UN Children's Rights Committee harshly criticizes Israel for unequal treatment of Arab and Arab Bedouin children. Haifa: Adalah: www.adalah.org/en/content/view/8178.

Aitken, S. 2015. Approaches to human geography. In *Approaches to Human Geography*. London: Sage Publishing: https://doi.org/10.4135/9781446215432.

Aizer, A., and F. Cunha. 2012. The production of human capital: endowments, investments and fertility. NBER Working Papers 18429. National Bureau of Economic Research, Inc., Cambridge, MA.

Alderson, P., and M. John. 2008. *Young Children's Rights: Exploring Beliefs, Principles and Practice*. 2nd edition. London: Jessica Kingsley.

Alston, P. 1995. *The United Nations and Human Rights*. Oxford University Press.

Allars, M. 2001. Citizenship rights, review rights and contractualism. *Law in Context* 18: 79.

Alston, P. 2015. "The World Bank is a human rights-free zone" – UN expert on extreme poverty expresses deep concern: www.ohchr.org/en/NewsEvents/Pages/DisplayNews.aspx?NewsID=16517&LangID=E.

Alston, P., and J. Tobin. 2005. Laying the foundations for children's rights: an independent study of some key legal and institutional aspects of the impact of the Convention on the Rights of the Child. Ser. Innocenti Insight 10. Florence: UNICEF Innocenti Research Centre.

Ammerman, N. (ed.). 2006. *Everyday Religion: Observing Modern Religious Lives.* Oxford University Press: www.oxfordscholarship.com/view/10.1093/acprof:oso/9780195305418.001.0001/acprof-9780195305418.

Archard, D. 2014a. *Children: Rights and Childhood.* Abingdon: Routledge.

Archard, D. 2014b. Insults, free speech and offensiveness. *Journal of Applied Philosophy*: https://doi.org/10.1111/japp.12048.

Arendt, H. 1949. The rights of man. *Modern Review* 3 (1): 24–36.

Arendt, H. 1951. *The Origins of Totalitarianism.* New York: Schocken Books.

Aristotle. 1994 [350 BCE]. *Politics.* Trans. B. Jowett. Cambridge, MA: MIT Press: http://classics.mit.edu/Aristotle/politics.1.one.html.

Aromaa, K., and M. Heiskanen (eds.). 2008. *Crime and Criminal Justice Systems in Europe and North America 1995–2004.* European Institute for Crime Prevention and Control, affiliated with the United Nations (HEUNI). Publication no. 55.

Balagopalan, S. 2014. *Inhabiting "Childhood": Children, Labour and Schooling in Postcolonial India.* New York: Palgrave Macmillan: https://doi.org/10.1057/9781137316790.

Barnes, A. 2012. CRC's performance of the child as developing. In *Law and Childhood Studies.* Ed. Michael Freeman. Oxford University Press, pp. 392–418.

Becker, H. S. 1986. *Writing for Social Scientists*. University of Chicago Press.

Benhabib, S. 1999. Citizens, residents, and aliens in a changing world. *Social Research* 66 (3): 709–44.

Benhabib, S. 2000 (2012). *The Rights of Others*. Cambridge University Press.

Bentley, K. A. 2005. Can there be any universal children's rights? *The International Journal of Human Rights* 9 (1): 107–23: https://doi.org/10.1080/13642980500032370.

Betcherman, G., J. Fares, A. Luinstra, and R. Prouty. 2004. Child labor, education, and children's rights (English). Social Protection Discussion Paper series SP 0412. Washington, DC: World Bank: http://documents. worldbank.org/curated/en/721061468762634105/Child-labor-education-and-childrens-rights.

Boyle, E. 2002. *Female Genital Cutting*. Baltimore, MD: Johns Hopkins University Press.

Boyle, E., and M. Kim. 2009. International human rights law, global economic reforms, and child survival and development rights outcomes. *Law Society Review* 43 (3): 455–90.

Boyle, E., and S. Preves. 2000. National legislating as international process: the case of anti-female-genital-cutting laws. *Law Society Review* 34: 401–32.

Boyle, E., and M. Thompson. 2001. National politics and resort to the European Commission on Human Rights. *Law Society Review* 35: 321–44.

Bromley, P. 2014. Legitimacy and the contingent diffusion of world culture: diversity and human rights in social science textbooks, divergent cross-national patterns (1970–2008). *Canadian Journal of Sociology* 39 (1): 1–44.

Chemerinsky, E. 2007. The state-created danger doctrine. *Touro Law Review* 23: 1–26.

Children's Rights Alliance for England. 2018. *State of*

Children's Rights 2018. London: Children's Rights Alliance for England.

Children's Rights Information Network. 2016. *Rights, Remedies, and Representation: Global Report on Access to Justice for Children*. London: Children's Rights Information Network.

Chinkin, C. 2006. Health and human rights. *Public Health* 2006-suppl. 1: 52–60.

Chunli, X. 2006. Migrant children and the right to compulsory education in China. *Asia-Pacific Journal on Human Rights and the Law* 2: 29–74.

Clark, R. 2010. Technical and institutional states: loose coupling in the human rights sector of the world polity. *Sociological Quarterly* 51: 65–95.

Close, P. 2014. *Child Labour in Global Society*. Somerville, MA: Emerald Publishing.

Cockburn, T. 1998. Children and citizenship in Britain: a case for a socially interdependent model of citizenship. *Childhood* 5 (1): 99–117: https://doi.org/10.1177/0907568298005001007.

Cohen, C. 1990. The role of nongovernmental organizations in the drafting of the Convention on the Rights of the Child. *Human Rights Quarterly* 12 (1): 137–47: https://doi.org/10.2307/762172.

Cohen, C. 2006. The role of the United States in the drafting of the Convention on the Rights of the Child. *Emory International Law Review* 20: 185–98.

Cole, W. 2005. Sovereignty relinquished? Explaining commitment to the international human rights covenants. *American Sociological Review* 70: 472–95.

Cole, W. 2009. Hard and soft commitments to human rights treaties, 1966–2000. *Sociological Forum* 24: 563–88.

Cole, W. 2012. Human rights as myth and ceremony?

Reevaluating the effectiveness of human rights treaties, 1981 to 2007. *American Journal of Sociology* 117 (4): 1131–71.

Cole, W. 2013. Strong walk and cheap talk: the effect of the International Covenant of Economic, Social, and Cultural Rights on Policies and Practices. *Social Forces* 92 (1): 165–94.

Collins, P. H. 1990. Black feminist thought. In *Social Theory Re-Wired: New Connections to Classical and Contemporary Perspectives*. 2nd edition. Abingdon: Routledge: https://doi.org/10.4324/9781315775357.

Darling-Hammond, L., L. Flook, C. Cook-Harvey, B. Barron, and D. Osher. 2020. Implications for educational practice of the science of learning and development. *Applied Developmental Science*: https://doi.org/10.1080/10888691.2018.1537791.

Deflem, M., and S. Chicoine. 2011. The sociological discourse on human rights. *Development and Society* 40 (1): 101–15.

De Sousa, M. 2018. Kailash Satyarthi: fighting for children's rights, one step at a time. *The UNESCO Courier* 1: 7–10: https://en.unesco.org/courier/january-march-2018/kailash-satyarthi-fighting-children-s-rights-one-step-time.

Dobbin, F., B. Simmons, and G. Garrett. 2007. The global diffusion of public policies. *Annual Review of Sociology* 33: 449–72.

Donnelly, J. 1984. Cultural relativism and universal human rights. *Human Rights Quarterly* 6 (4): 400–19: https://doi.org/10.2307/762182.

Donnelly, J. 2013. *Universal Human Rights in Theory and Practice*. Ithaca: Cornell University Press.

Dworkin, R. 1977. *Taking Rights Seriously*. Cambridge, MA: Harvard University Press.

Dwyer, J. 1994. Primum non tacere: an ethics of speaking up. *Hastings Center Report* 24: 13–18: https://doi.org/10.2307/3562380.

Edin, K., and M. Kefalas. 2005. *Promises I Can Keep: Why Poor Women Put Motherhood before Marriage.* Berkeley: University of California Press.

End Corporal Punishment. 2020: https://endcorporal punishment.org.

Esping-Andersen, G. 1990. *Three Worlds of Welfare Capitalism.* Princeton University Press.

European Commission. 2020. Missing children and child alert mechanisms: https://ec.europa.eu/info/policies/justice-and-fundamental-rights/rights-child/missing-children-and-child-alert-mechanisms_en.

FAO (Food and Agriculture Organization of the United Nations). n.d. Child labour in agriculture: www.fao.org/childlabouragriculture/en.

Fass, P. S. 2011. How history has shaped children's rights. *Annals of the American Academy of Political and Social Science* Feb. 25: www.aapss.org/news/paula-fass-how-history-has-shaped-childrens-rights.

Feldman, S. S., and T. Quatman. 1988. Factors influencing age expectations for adolescent autonomy: a study of early adolescents and parents. *The Journal of Early Adolescence* 8 (4): 325–43: https://doi.org/10.1177/0272431688084002.

Fieldhouse, E., M. Tranmer, and A. Russell. 2007. Something about young people or something about elections? Electoral participation of young people in Europe: evidence from a multilevel analysis of the European Social Survey. *European Journal of Political Research*: https://doi.org/10.1111/j.1475-6765.2007.00713.x.

Fink, A. 2003. What is a survey? When do you use one? In A. Fink, *The Survey Handbook.* Thousand Oaks, CA: SAGE Publications, Inc., pp. 1–29: https://doi.org/10.4135/9781412986328.

Fink, A. 2013. *How to Conduct Surveys*. Thousand Oaks, CA: SAGE Publications.

Fortin, J. 2009. *Children's Rights and the Developing Law*. Cambridge University Press: https://doi.org/10.1017/CBO9781139168625.

Foucault, M. 1975. *Discipline and Punish*. New York: Random House.

Foucault, M. 2003. *Society Must Be Defended*. London: Picador.

Foucault, M. 2003/6. *Psychiatric Power: Lectures at the Collège de France, 1973–1974*. New York: Palgrave Macmillan. Orignally published as *Pouvoir psychiatrique: cours au Collège de France, 1973–1974*. Paris: Seuil/Gallimard.

Freeman, M. 1998. The right to be heard. *Adoption & Fostering* 22 (4): 50–9: https://doi.org/10.1177/030857599802200408.

Freeman, M. 2000. The future of children's rights. *Children and Society* 14: 277–93.

Gobetti, D. 1997. Humankind as a system: private and public agency at the origins of modern liberalism. In *Public and Private Thought and Practice*. Ed. J. Weintraub and K. Kumar. University of Chicago Press, pp. 103–32.

Gran, B. 2009. The rights of the child. In *The Leading Rogue State: The US and Human Rights*. Ed. J. Blau, A. Moncada, C. Zimmer and D. Brunsma. Boulder, CO: Paradigm Publishers, pp. 47–50.

Gran, B. 2011. The roles of independent children's rights institutions in implementing the CRC. In *Children's Rights: From 20th Century Visions to 21st Century Implementation?* Ed. J. Williams and A. Invernizzi. Farnham: Ashgate, pp. 219–37.

Gran, B. 2020. Children's ombudspersons in the United States. *Societies Without Borders* 14 (1): https://scholarly-commons.law.case.edu/swb/vol14/iss1/9.

Gran, B., and D. M. Aliberti. 2003. The office of the children's ombudsperson: children's rights and social-policy innovation. *International Journal of the Sociology of Law* 31 (2): 89–106.

Gregg, B. 2011. Human rights as social construction. In *Human Rights as Social Construction*. Cambridge University Press.

Grover, S. C. 2010. *Young People's Human Rights and the Politics of Voting Age*. New York: Springer.

Guggenheim, M. 2005. *What's Wrong with Children's Rights?* Cambridge, MA: Harvard University Press.

Gusó, M., A. Saporiti, M. Rago, D. Grignoli, M. González, A. Mancini, M. Sadurní, F. Ferrucci, C. Alsinet, C. Figuer, C. Rostan, and F. Casas. 2006. Children's rights from the point of view of children, their parents and their teachers: a comparative study between Catalonia (Spain) and Molise (Italy). *The International Journal of Children's Rights* 14: 1–75: https://doi.org/10.1163/157181806776614336.

Hafner-Burton, E. 2005. Trading human rights: how preferential trade agreements influence government repression. *International Organization* 59: 593–629.

Hafner-Burton, E. 2008. Sticks and stones: naming and shaming the human rights enforcement problem. *International Organization* 62: 689–716.

Hafner-Burton, E., and K. Tsutsui. 2005. Human rights in a globalizing world: the paradox of empty promises. *American Journal of Sociology* 110: 1373–411.

Hafner-Burton, E., and K. Tsutsui. 2007. Justice lost! The failure of international human rights law to matter where needed most. *The Journal of Peace Research* 44 (4): 407–25.

Hafner-Burton, E., K. Tsutsui, and J. W. Meyer. 2008. International human rights law and the politics of legitimation: repressive states and human rights treaties. *International Sociology* 23: 115–41.

Hagan, J., and R. Levi. 2007. Justiciability as field effect: when sociology meets human rights. *Sociological Forum* 22: 372–80.

Hallett, T., and M. J. Ventresca. 2006. Inhabited institutions: social interactions and organizational forms in Gouldner's *Patterns of Industrial Bureaucracy*. *Theory & Society* 35: 213–36: https://doi.org/10.1007/s11186-006-9003-z.

Hashemi, M. 2012. Social mobility among poor youth in Iran. Dissertation, Department of Sociology, University of California–Berkeley.

Hathaway, O. 2003. The cost of commitment. *Stanford Law Review* 55: 1821–62.

Hathaway, O. 2007. Why do countries commit to human rights treaties? *Journal of Conflict Resolution* 51 (4): 588–621.

Hernandez, D. J. 1993. The historical transformation of childhood, children's statistics, and social policy. *Childhood*: https://doi.org/10.1177/090756829300100401.

Hertel, S., and K. Libal. 2011. *Human Rights in the United States: Beyond Exceptionalism*. Cambridge University Press.

Hillman, A., and E. Jenkner. 2004. Educating children in poor countries. International Monetary Fund, Economic Issues 33: www.imf.org/external/pubs/ft/issues/issues33/index.htm.

Hillman, J., M. Taylor, T. Pearson, J. Cook, N. Thomas, A. Crowley, R. Pugh-Dungey, H. France, C. Jenkins, M. Cook, and B. Sawyers. 2010. Evaluating the Children's Commissioner for Wales: report of a participatory research study. *The International Journal of Children's Rights* 18 (1): 19–52: https://doi.org/10.1163/092755609X12513491775651.

Hirsch, P., and M. Lounsbury. 2015. Toward a more critical and "powerful" institutionalism. *Journal of Management Inquiry* 24 (1): 96–9: https://doi.org/10.1177/1056492614545297.

Hohfeld, W. N. 1917. Fundamental legal conceptions as applied in judicial reasoning. *The Yale Law Journal*: https://doi.org/10.2307/786270.

Howard-Hassmann, R. E. 2000. Multiculturalism, human rights, and cultural relativism: Canadian civic leaders discuss women's rights and gay and lesbian rights. *Netherlands Quarterly of Human Rights* 18 (4): 493–514: https://doi.org/10.1177/092405190001800403.

Huang, Y. 2013. *Confucius: A Guide for the Perplexed*. London: A&C Black.

Human Rights Watch. 2010. Disability rights. Accessed May 17, 2020: www.hrw.org/topic/disability-rights.

Human Rights Watch. March 22, 2018. Lebanon: schools discriminate against children with disabilities. Accessed May 17, 2020: www.hrw.org/news/2018/03/22/lebanon-schools-discriminate-against-children-disabilities#.

Human Rights Watch. 2019. Nigeria: people with mental health conditions abused, chained. Accessed May 21, 2020: www.hrw.org/news/2019/11/11/nigeria-people-mental-health-conditions-chained-abused.

Hutchinson, A., and P. Monahan. 1984. Law, politics, and the critical legal scholars: the unfolding drama of American legal thought. *Stanford Law Review* 36 (1/2): 199–245: https://doi.org/10.2307/1228683.

IMF (International Monetary Fund). 2018a. Budgeting for gender and children's rights in Burkina Faso, June 15: https://blog-pfm.imf.org/pfmblog/2018/06/-budgeting-for-gender-and-childrens-rights-in-burkina-faso-.html.

IMF (International Monetary Fund). 2018b. *Building a Shared Future: IMF Annual Report*. Washington, DC: IMF.

International Labour Organization. 2003. *Investing in Every Child*. Geneva, Switzerland: ILO.

International Labour Organization. 2004. Child labor,

education, and children's rights: www.ilo.org/caribbean/projects/WCMS_308202/lang--en/index.htm.

International Labour Organization. 2017a. Promotion and protection of the rights of children: www.ilo.org/newyork/at-the-un/general-assembly/general-assembly-third-committee/promotion-and-protection-of-the-rights-of-children/lang--en/index.htm.

International Labour Organization. 2017b. *Global Estimates of Child Labour*. Geneva, Switzerland: ILO.

IOM and UNICEF. 2015. Data brief: migration of children to Europe. Berlin: Global Migration Data Analysis Centre.

Isin, E. F., and P. K. Wood. 1999. *Citizenship and Identity*. Thousand Oaks, CA: Sage.

Janoski, T. 1998. *Citizenship and Civil Society*. Cambridge University Press.

Janoski, T. 2012. The ironies of citizenship: naturalization and integration in industrialized countries. In *The Ironies of Citizenship: Naturalization and Integration in Industrialized Countries*: https://doi.org/10.1017/CBO9780511779206.

Janoski, T., and B. Gran. 2002. Political citizenship: foundations of rights. In E. F. Isin and B. S. Turner, *Handbook of Citizenship Studies*. London: Sage Publishing, pp. 13–52: https://doi.org/10.4135/9781848608276.

The Justice Foundation. n.d. The Justice Foundation supports parental rights in education: https://thejusticefoundation.org/info/parental-rights.

Kagan, R. 1991. Adversarial legalism and American government. *Journal of Policy Analysis and Management* 10 (3): 369–406: https://doi.org/10.2307/3325322.

Kagan, R. 2003. *Adversarial Legalism*. Cambridge, MA: Harvard University Press.

Kagan, R. 2019. *Adversarial Legalism*. 2nd edition. Cambridge, MA: Harvard University Press.

Kennedy, C., and K. Covell. 2009. Violating the rights of the child through inadequate sexual health education. *International Journal of Children's Rights* 17: 143–54.

Kessler-Harris, A. 2003. In pursuit of economic citizenship. *Social Politics: International Studies in Gender, State & Society* 10 (2): 157–75: https://doi.org/10.1093/sp/jxg008.

Kim, M., and E. Boyle. 2012. Neoliberalism, transnational education norms, and education spending in the developing world, 1983–2004. *Law & Social Inquiry* 37 (2): 367–94.

Kim, M., E. Boyle, W. Longhofer, and H. N. Brehm. 2013. When do laws matter? Marriage laws, child's rights, and adolescent fertility, 1989–2007. *Law Society Review* 47 (3): 589–619.

Kingsley, P. September 26, 2018a. In Britain, even children are feeling the effects of austerity. *New York Times*: www.nytimes.com/2018/09/26/world/europe/uk-austerity-child-poverty.html.

Kingsley, P. November 16, 2018b. British austerity is "inflicting unnecessary misery," U.N. poverty expert says. *New York Times*: www.nytimes.com/2018/11/16/world/europe/uk-un-poverty-austerity.html.

Langille, D., P. Andreou, R. Beazley, and M. Delaney. 1998. Sexual health knowledge of students at a high school in Nova Scotia. *Canadian Journal of Public Health. Revue canadienne de santé publique* 89: 85–9: https://doi.org/10.1007/BF03404394.

Langlaude, S. 2007. *The Right of the Child to Religious Freedom in International Law*. Leiden: Brill–Nijhoff: https://doi.org/10.1163/ej.9789004162662.i-293.

Lansdown, G. 1994. Children's rights. In *Children's Childhoods*

Observed and Experienced. Ed. B. Myall. London: Falmer Press, pp. 33–44.

Lansdown, G., S. R. Jimerson, and R. Shahroozi. 2014. Children's rights and school psychology: children's right to participation. *Journal of School Psychology* 52 (1): 3–12.

Lareau, A. 2011. *Unequal Childhoods: Race, Class, and Family Life*. Berkeley: University of California Press.

Lareau, A., and J. M. Calarco. 2012. Class, cultural capital, and institutions: the case of families and schools. In *Facing Social Class: How Societal Rank Influences Interaction*. Ed. S. T. Fiske and H. R. Markus. New York: Russell Sage Foundation, pp. 61–86.

Launcer, J. 2009. No place for children. *British Journal of General Practice* 58 (564): 543.

Library of Congress. n.d. Jacob Riis: www.loc.gov/exhibits/jacob-riis/biography.html.

Link, B. G., and J. Phelan. 1995. Social conditions as fundamental causes of disease. *Journal of Health and Social Behavior*: https://doi.org/10.2307/2626958.

Linnarsson, A., and V. Sedletzki. 2014. Independent human rights institutions for children: an actor for the protection of children's rights during armed conflict? *Human Rights Quarterly* 36: 447–72.

Long, M. D., and R. Sephton. 2011. Rethinking the "best interests" of the child: voices from Aboriginal Child and Family Welfare practitioners. *Australian Social Work* 64: 112–96.

Lord, C. 1984. *Aristotle's Politics. Translated with an Introduction, Notes and Glossary*. Chicago and London: University of Chicago Press.

Lux, A. 2020. Independent Children's Rights Institutions: their contribution to human rights of children. *Societies Without Borders* 14 (1): https://scholarlycommons.law.case.edu/swb/vol14/iss1/2.

Mann, M. 1987. Ruling class strategies and citizenship. *Sociology* 21 (3): 339–54: https://doi.org/10.1177/0038038 587021003003.

Mares, I. 2015. *From Open Secrets to Secret Voting: Democratic Electoral Reforms and Voter Autonomy*. New York: Cambridge University Press.

Marsh, D., T. O'Toole, and S. Jones. 2007. *Young People and Politics in the UK: Apathy or Alienation?* London: Palgrave Macmillan.

Marshall, T. H. 1949. Citizenship and social class. *The British Journal of Sociology*: https://doi.org/10.2307/587460.

Marshall, T. H. 1950. *Citizenship and Social Class*. Cambridge at the University Press.

Matthews, G. B. 1996. *The Philosophy of Childhood*. Cambridge, MA: Harvard University Press.

Mayo Clinic. 2018. Circumcision (male): www.mayoclinic. org/tests-procedures/circumcision/about/pac-20393550.

McCluskey, G., S. Riddell, and E. Weedon. 2015. Children's rights, school exclusion and alternative educational provision. *International Journal of Inclusive Education* 19 (60): 595–607: https://doi.org/10.1080/13603116.2014.96 1677.

Melton, G. B. 1980. Children's concepts of their rights. *Journal of Clinical Child Psychology*: https://doi. org/10.1080/15374418009532985.

Merry, S. E. 2006. *Human Rights and Gender Violence*. University of Chicago Press.

Meyer, J. 1980. The world polity and the authority of the nation-state. In *Studies of the Modern World System*. Ed. A. Bergesen. New York: Academic, pp. 109–37.

Meyer, J., and B. Rowan. 1977. Institutionalized organizations. *American Journal of Sociology* 83 (2): 340–63.

Meyer, J., and B. Rowan. 1991. Institutional organizations:

formal structure as myth and ceremony. In *The New Institutionalism in Organizational Analysis*. Ed. Walter W. Powell and Paul J. Dimaggio. University of Chicago Press, pp. 41–62.

Miles, E. 1968. Organizations and integration in international systems. *International Studies Quarterly* 12 (2): 196–224: doi:10.2307/3013501.

Minow, M. 2003. *Partners, not Rivals*. Boston: Beacon.

Mortorano, B. 2014. The consequences of the recent economic crisis and government reactions for children. Innocenti Working Paper 2014–05. Florence: UNICEF Office of Research.

Moyn, Samuel. May 16, 2016. Rights v. duties. *Boston Review*: http://bostonreview.net/books-ideas/samuel-moyn-rights-duties.

Mutcherson, K. M. 2006. Minor discrepancies: forging a common understanding of adolescent competence in healthcare decision-making and criminal responsibility. *Nevada Law Journal* 6 (3), Article 20: 927–65: https://scholars.law.unlv.edu/nlj/vol6/iss3/20.

Nauck, B. 1994. Note, implications of the United States Ratification of the United Nations Convention on the Rights of the Child: civil rights, the Constitution and the family. *Cleveland State Law Review* 42: 675.

Ochieng, N. T., K. Wilson, C. J. Derrick, and N. Mukherjee. 2018. The use of focus group discussion methodology: insights from two decades of application in conservation. *Methods in Ecology and Evolution* 9: 20–32: https://doi.org/10.1111/2041-210X.12860.

Organisation for Economic Co-operation and Development. 2020. Education spending (indicator): https://doi.org/10.1787/ca274bac-en.

Organization of American States Inter-American Children's Institute. 2007. Políticas públicas y derechos humanos del niño. Montevideo, Uruguay: OAS Inter-American Children's Institute.

Osler, C., and A. H. Osler. 2002. Inclusion, exclusion and children's rights: a case study of a student with Asperger Syndrome. *None* 7 (1): 35–54.

Papacostas, A. 2008. European Commission: Flash Eurobarometer 235 (The rights of the child). The GALLUP Organisation, Brussels. GESIS Data Archive, Cologne. ZA4814 Data file Version 1.0.0: https://doi.org/10.4232/1.4814.

Papacostas, A. 2009. European Commission: Flash Eurobarometer 273 (The rights of the child). The GALLUP Organisation, Brussels. GESIS Data Archive, Cologne. ZA4 987 Data file Version 1.0.0: https://doi.org/10.4232/1.4987.

Pearson, S. J. 2011. *The Rights of the Defenseless*. University of Chicago Press.

Pupavac, V. 2011. Punishing childhoods: contradictions in children's rights and global governance. *Journal of Intervention and Statebuilding* 5 (3): 285–312: https://doi.org/10.1080/17502977.2011.566486.

Qvortrup, J. 2014. Sociology: societal structure, development of childhood, and the well-being of children. In *Handbook of Child Well-Being*. Ed. A. Ben-Arieh, F. Casas, I. Frønes, and J. Korbin. Dordrecht: Springer, pp. 663–707.

Raudenbush, D. T. 2012. Race and interactions on public transportation: social cohesion and the production of common norms and a collective black identity. *Symbolic Interaction*: https://doi.org/10.1002/SYMB.36.

Reynaert, D., M. Bouverne-De Bie, and S. Vandevelde. 2012. Between "believers" and "opponents": critical discussions on children's rights. *International Journal of Children's Rights*: https://doi.org/10.1163/157181812X626417.

Reynolds, P., O. Nieuwenhuys, and K. Hanson. 2006.

Refractions of children's rights in development practice: a view from anthropology – introduction. *Childhood*: https://doi.org/10.1177/0907568206067476.

Ridgely, S. B. 2011. *The Study of Children in Religions: A Methods Handbook*. New York University Press.

Riley-Smith, B. 2016. Making children attend Christian school assemblies undermines human rights, United Nations warns. *Telegraph*, June 9: www.telegraph.co.uk/news/2016/06/09/making-children-attend-christian-school-assemblies-undermines-hu.

Romany, C. 1993. Women as aliens: a feminist critique of the public/private distinction in international human rights law. *Harvard Human Rights Journal* 6: 87.

Romero, M. 2020. Sociology engaged in social justice. *American Sociological Review*: https://doi.org/10.1177/0003122419893677.

Salazar-Volkmann, C. 2005. 30 years after the war: children, families, and rights in Vietnam. *International Journal of Law, Policy, and the Family* 19 (1): 23–46: https://doi.org/10.1093/lawfam/ebi002.

Samuelsen, R. J. 2011. Vil at barn skal bo hos mor eller far. *Aftenposten* Oct. 20: www.aftenposten. no/norge/Vil-at-barn-skal-bo-hos-mor-eller-far-319546b.html.

Savery, L. 2007. *Engendering the State*. London: Routledge.

Save the Children and Food and Agricultural Organization. 2009. Children and women's rights to property and inheritance in Mozambique. Save the Children in Mozambique.

Schutt, R. 2018. *Investigating the Social World*. 9th edition. Thousand Oaks, CA: SAGE Publishing.

Sealander, J. 2003. *The Failed Century of the Child: Governing America's Young in the Twentieth Century*. Cambridge University Press.

Seneviratne, D., and F. Mariam. 2011. Home truths: children's rights in institutional care in Sri Lanka. In *Children's Rights and International Development: Lessons and Challenges from the Field*: https://doi.org/10.1057/9780230119253.

Sharkey, P. T., N. Tirado-Strayer, A. V. Papachristos, and C. C. Raver. 2012. The effect of local violence on children's attention and impulse control. *American Journal of Public Health*: https://doi.org/10.2105/AJPH.2012.300789.

Shier, H. 2001. Pathways to participation: openings, opportunities and obligations. *Children & Society* 15: 107–17.

Skelton, T. 2010. Taking young people as political actors seriously: opening the borders of political geography. *Area* 42 (2): 145–51: www.jstor.org/stable/27801455.

Sloam, J., and M. Henn. 2019. Rejuvenating politics: young political participation in a changing world. In *Youthquake 2017*. Ed. James Sloam and Matt Henn. Palgrave Studies in Young People and Politics. London: Palgrave Macmillan, pp. 17–42.

Soh, C. S. 2008. *The Comfort Women*. University of Chicago Press.

Søvig, K. H. 2019. Incorporating the Convention in Norwegian law. In *Children's Rights in Norway*. Ed. Malcolm Langford, Marit Skivenes, and Karl Harald Søvig. Oslo: Universitetsforlaget, pp. 269–99: https://doi.org/10.18261/9788215031415-2019-10.

Soysal, Y. 1994. *The Limits of Citizenship*. Cambridge University Press.

Spring, J. 2018. Strangers in our midst: the political philosophy of immigration. *Contemporary Political Theory* 17: 240–3: https://doi.org/10.1057/s41296-017-0147-6.

Stevens, J. 1999. *Reproducing the State*. Princeton University Press.

Stinchcombe, A. L. 1965. Social structure and organizations.

Advances in Strategic Management: https://doi.org/10.1016/S0956-5221(03)00039-3.

Stinchcombe, A. L. 1997. On the virtues of the old institutionalism. *Annual Review of Sociology* 23 (1): 1–18.

Straus, M., R. J. Gelles, and S. Steinmetz. 2006. *Behind Closed Doors*. New York: Routledge.

Svoboda, J. Steven. 2013. Promoting genital autonomy by exploring commonalities between male, female, intersex, and cosmetic female genital cutting. *Global Discourse* 3 (2): 237–55: https://doi.org/10.1080/23269995.2013.804757.

Taylor, C. 2012. Foucault and familial power. *Hypatia* 27 (1): 201–18: www.jstor.org/stable/41328905.

Taylor, N., A. Smith, and M. Gollop. 2008. New Zealand children and young people's perspectives on citizenship. *The International Journal of Children's Rights* 16: 195–210: https://doi.org/10.1163/157181808X301791.

Therborn, G. 1996. Child politics: dimensions and perspectives. *Childhood* 3 (1): 29–44: https://doi.org/10.1177/0907568296003001003.

Thomas, N., B. Gran, and K. Hanson. 2011. An independent voice for children's rights in Europe? The role of independent children's rights institutions in the EU. *International Journal of Children's Rights* 19 (3): 429–49: https://doi.org/10.1163/157181811X584550.

Thorne, B. 1993. Gender play: girls and boys in school. *Social Forces*: https://doi.org/10.2307/2580577.

Tibet Watch. 2020. UN Committee on the Rights of the Child: www.tibetwatch.org/crc.

Tilly, C. 1983. Flows of capital and forms of industry in Europe, 1500–1900. *Theory and Society* 12: 123–42: https://doi.org/10.1007/BF00157009.

Timpson, E., Minister of State for Vulnerable Children and Families. October 17, 2016. *Commitment to UNCRC: Written Statement* – HLWS197.

Todres, J., M. Wojcik, and C. Revaz (eds.). 2006. *The U.N. Convention on the Rights of the Child: An Analysis of Treaty Provisions and Implications of U.S. Ratification.* Leiden: Brill Academic Publishers.

Tremblay, P. R., and J. A. McMorrow. 2013. Lawyers and the new institutionalism. *University of St. Thomas Law Journal* 8 (1): 568–92.

Turner, B. S. 2006. *Vulnerability and Human Rights.* University Park: Pennsylvania State University Press: https://doi.org/10.1163/187219107x216726.

Tushnet, M. 1991. Critical Legal Studies: A Political History. *Yale Law Journal* 100: 1515–44.

Tuttle, C. 2018. *Children in the Industrial Revolution.* Oxford Bibliographies. Oxford University Press.

UN Committee on Economic, Social and Cultural Rights. 2020. General Comment No. 25 (2020) on Science and Economic, Social and Cultural Rights (Articles 15 (1) (b), (2), (3) and (4) of the International Covenant on Economic, Social and Cultural Rights).

UNICEF. 2015. Levels and trends in child malnutrition: key findings of the 2015 edition. New York: UNICEF.

UNICEF. 2017. Orphans: https://www.unicef.org/media/media_45279.html.

United Nations. 2015. UN news: UN lauds Somalia as country ratifies landmark children's rights treaty: https://news.un.org/en/story/2015/01/488692-un-lauds-somalia-country-ratifies-landmark-childrens-rights-treaty.

United Nations. 2020. About the Sustainable Development Goals. Accessed May 17, 2020: www.un.org/sustainabledevelopment/sustainable-development-goals.

United Nations. n.d. The International Bill of Human Rights: https://www.ohchr.org/Documents/Publications/Compilation1.1en.pdf.

United Nations Children's Fund. 2006. *Child and Youth Participation Guide*. Bangkok: UNICEF East Asia and Pacific Regional Office.

United Nations Children's Fund. 2013. *Championing Children's Rights*. Florence: UNICEF.

United Nations Children's Fund. 2016. *Female Genital Mutilation/Cutting: A Global Concern*: Data.unicef.org.

United Nations Children's Fund. n.d.a. *Adolescent Development and Participation*: www.unicef.org/adolescence/cypguide/41190_governance.html.

United Nations Children's Fund. n.d.b. UNICEF is the Custodian or Co-Custodian of 17 SDG indicators: https://data.unicef.org/children-sustainable-development-goals.

United Nations Children's Fund. n.d.c. What we do: www.unicef.org/what-we-do.

United Nations Children's Fund, WHO, and World Bank. n.d. Prevalence of stunting, height for age (% of children under 5). Joint child malnutrition estimates (JME). Aggregation is based on UNICEF, WHO, and the World Bank harmonized dataset (adjusted, comparable data) and methodology: https://data.worldbank.org/indicator/SH.STA.STNT.ZS.

United Nations Committee on the Rights of the Child. 2020. Working methods: www.ohchr.org/EN/HRBodies/CRC/Pages/WorkingMethods.aspx.

United Nations Educational, Scientific and Cultural Organization. 2016. UNESCO campus. Accessed May 26, 2020: https://en.unesco.org/events/unesco-campus.

United Nations Educational, Scientific and Cultural Organization. n.d. By youth, with youth, for youth: https://en.unesco.org/youth.

United Nations General Assembly, Human Rights Council. 2018. *Report of the Special Rapporteur on the Issue of Human*

Rights Obligations Relating to the Enjoyment of a Safe, Clean, Healthy and Sustainable Environment. A/HRC/37/58.

UN Population Fund. 2005. Human rights principles: https://www.unfpa.org/resources/human-rights-principles.

The US Commission on Civil Rights. 2018. *Public Education Funding Inequity.* Washington, DC: US Commission on Civil Rights.

US State Department. 2016. *2016 Country Reports on Human Rights Practices: Nigeria.* https://www.state.gov/reports/2016-country-reports-on-human-rights-practices/nigeria.

Van Bueren, G. 1998. *The International Law on the Rights of the Child.* Leiden: Martinus Nijhoff.

Van Deth, J. W., J. R. Montero, and A. Westholm. 2007. *Citizenship and Involvement in European Democracies: A Comparative Analysis. Abingdon: Routledge.*

Ventresca, M. 2002. Global policy fields: conflicts and settlements in the emergence of organized international attention to official statistics, 1853–1947. Institute for Policy Research Working Paper. Evanston, IL: Northwestern University.

Volkmann, C. S. 2005. 30 years after the war: children, families, and rights in Vietnam. *International Journal of Law, Policy, and the Family* 19 (1): 23–46: https://doi.org/10.1093/lawfam/ebi002.

Waibel, M. 2014. Interpretive communities in international law. In *Interpretation in International Law*. Ed. Andrea Bianchi, Daniel Peat, and Matthew Windsor. Oxford University Press, pp. 147–65: https://doi.org/10.1093/acprof:oso/9780198725749.003.0007.

Wakefield, S., and C. Wildeman. 2013. *Children of the Prison Boom.* Oxford University Press: https://doi.org/10.1093/acprof:oso/9780199989225.001.0001.

Wall, J. 2014. Why children and youth should have the right to vote: an argument for proxy-claim suffrage. *Children, Youth and Environments* 24 (1): 108–23.

Wall, J., and A. Dar. 2011. Children's political representation: the right to make a difference. *International Journal of Children's Rights* 19 (4): 595–612.

Wang, L. 2013. Towards cultural citizenship? Cultural rights and cultural policy in Taiwan. *Citizenship Studies* 17 (1): 92–110: https://doi.org/10.1080/13621025.2012.716213.

Watts, C. D. 2004. Asking adolescents: does a mature minor have a right to participate in health care decisions? *Hastings Women's Law Journal* 16: 221.

Welch, S., and P. Jones. 2018. *Rethinking Children's Rights*. New York: Bloomsbury.

Whittaker, A. 2018. How do child protection practitioners make decisions in real life situations? Lessons from the psychology of decision making. *British Journal of Social Work* 48 (7): 1967–84: https://doi.org/10.1093/bjsw/bcx145.

Willard, G. 1982. The "competence" of children: no longer all or none. *Journal of the American Academy of Child Psychiatry* 21 (2): 153–62: https://doi.org/10.1016/S0002-7138(09)60914-6.

Williams, P. 1992. *The Alchemy of Race and Rights*. Cambridge, MA: Harvard University Press.

Wilson, W. J. 1987. The truly disadvantaged. *Journal of Policy Analysis and Management*: https://doi.org/10.2307/3323400.

Woll, L. 2000. *The Convention on the Rights of the Child Impact Study*. Stockholm: Save the Children – Sweden.

World Bank. January 22, 2019. The education crisis: being in school is not the same as learning: www.worldbank.org/en/news/immersive-story/2019/01/22/pass-or-fail-how-can-the-world-do-its-homework.

World Bank. 2020. Low-birthweight babies (% of births). May 26: data.worldbank.org.

World Bank. n.d. Identification for development: http://pubdocs.worldbank.org/en/726141507833458171/ID4DBrochure101217.pdf.

World Health Organization. 2010. *Neonatal and Child Male Circumcision: A Global Review*. Geneva, Switzerland: WHO.

World Health Organization. 2014. Convention on the Rights of the Child: www.who.int/gender-equity-rights/news/rights-child-convention-anniversary/en.

World Health Organization. n.d. World Health Survey: www.who.int/healthinfo/survey/en.

World Justice Report. 2019. What the data says about criminal justice systems around the world: https://worldjusticeproject.org/news/what-data-says-about-criminal-justice-systems-around-world.

World Policy Analysis Center. n.d. World Policy Analysis Center: https://ph.ucla.edu/research/centers/world-policy-analysis-center.

Wotipka, C. M., and F. O. Ramirez. 2008. World society and human rights. In *The Global Diffusion of Markets and Democracy*. Ed. B. A. Simmons, F. Dobbin, and G. Garrett. Cambridge University Press, pp. 303–43.

Wotipka, C. M., and K. Tsutsui. 2008. Global human rights and state sovereignty: state ratification of international human rights treaties, 1965–2001. *Sociological Forum* 23: 724–54.

LEGAL CASES

Deshaney v. Winnebago County Department of Social Services, 489 U.S. 189 (1989).

Roper v. Simmons, 543 US 55 (2005).

Treaties

1924 Geneva Declaration of the Rights of the Child
1959 Declaration of the Rights of the Child
African Charter on the Rights and Welfare of the Child
European Convention on Human Rights
International Covenant on Civil and Political Rights (ICCPR)
International Covenant on Economic, Social and Cultural Rights (ICESCR)
United Nations Convention on the Elimination of All Forms of Discrimination against Women (CEDAW)
United Nations Convention on the Rights of People with Disabilities (CRPD)
United Nations Convention on the Rights of the Child (UNCRC)
United Nations International Convention on the Protection of the Rights of All Migrant Workers and Members of their Families (CMW)
Universal Declaration of Human Rights (UDHR)

Committees

African Committee of Experts on the Rights and Welfare of the Child
UN Committee on Economic, Social and Cultural Rights
UN Committee on Eliminating Discrimination against Women
UN Committee on the Protection of the Rights of All Migrant Workers and Members of their Families
UN Committee on the Rights of Children
UN Human Rights Committee

Index

Page numbers in *italics* refer to figures/tables.